ELLY SIENKIEWICZ

Baltimore Elegance

A New Approach to Classic Album Quilts

C&T PUBLISHING

© 2006 Eleanor Patton Hamilton Sienkiewicz

Publisher   Amy Marson

Editorial Director   Gailen Runge

Acquisitions Editor   Jan Grigsby

Editor   Lynn Koolish

Technical Editors   Joyce Lytle and Susan Nelsen

Copyeditor/Proofreader   Wordfirm Inc.

Cover Designer   Christina Jarumay

Design Director/Book Designer   Rose Wright (Graphic Productions)

Illustrator   Richard Shepard

Production Assistant   Kirstie L. Pettersen

Photography   Luke Mulks unless otherwise noted

Published by C&T Publishing, Inc., P.O. Box 1456, Lafayette, CA 94549

Front cover   *To Chris With Love* by Angie Witting

Back cover   *Quiet Moments* by Betty F. Augustine
Album Block Carrying Case, adapted and made by Janice Vanine

Library of Congress Cataloging-in-Publication Data

Sienkiewicz, Elly.

Baltimore elegance : a new approach to classic album quilts / Elly Sienkiewicz.

p. cm.

Includes index.

ISBN-13: 978-1-57120-274-1 (paper trade)

ISBN-10: 1-57120-274-9 (paper trade)

1. Patchwork--Patterns. 2. Appliqué--Patterns. 3. Album quilts--Maryland--Baltimore. I. Title.

TT835.S5144 2006

746.46'041--dc22

2006002797

Printed in China

10 9 8 7 6 5 4 3 2 1

Table of Contents

Dove and Anchor block, by Bette F. Augustine
(Reproduction Pattern 3, page 152)

Dedication

Jana Sophia Sienkiewicz was born March 20, 2005, to our Donald and Katja in Arlington, Massachusetts. Colter Meadows Sienkiewicz was born May 23, 2005, to our Alex and Holly in Missoula, Montana. This book is dedicated to you, dear and magical grandchildren—you who when this book was being written were a yearning in your parents' hearts; you who were loved and longed for years before your birth. You are our childhood's dream and our old-age blessing, now come true! All our love, Grandmother and Grandfather Sienkiewicz.

Acknowledgments

Needleartists created the quilts that so beautifully illustrate this book. Without them, this book would never have been. Thank you each, from the bottom of my heart, for sharing your time and talent with us all.

Thank you more than words can say to Janice Vaine, who developed the designs, worked up the fabric models, and prepared the preliminary instructions for many of the small projects, so that you, Dear Reader, might make these smashing stitcheries your very own. Thanks as well to Jo Anne Maddelena, who permitted us to modify her original Album Block Carrying Case from *Papercuts and Plenty: Volume Three of Baltimore Beauties and Beyond*.

My gratitude to my loyal publisher, C&T Publishing, and all who worked so hard to bring this book to life!

My appreciation to my sponsors, Harvey and Ken Kaufman, and the talented staff at Robert Kaufman Fabrics, manufacturers of my Beyond Baltimore and Spoken Without a Word fabric collections. A special thank-you to Design Director Evie Ashworth, who "learned Baltimore" to oversee the skillful beyond-Baltimore design of the fabrics.

Thank you as well to my other gracious corporate sponsors—Hobbs Bonded Fibers, DMC Corporation, YLI Threads, The Appliqué Society, Bernina of America, and the Fairfield Processing Corporation—for their generous support.

In addition, my thanks to: My mother, Eileen Mary Clare-Patton Hamilton-Wigner, who at 90 still blesses me with her wisdom and love. My daughter-in-law, Katja Sienkiewicz, for her candid project and author photos.

Each member of the Elly Sienkiewicz Appliqué Academy LLC® who contributed the vintage inscriptions and quotable verses with which this book's blocks can be inscribed. Hugs and thanks to Bette Augustine, Academy Administrator, for all she is and does.

The hospitable proprietors of my coffee café writing "offices": Books by the Bay in Lewes Beach, Delaware, Starbucks, Caribou Coffee, and Barnes & Noble in Washington, D.C., and Bethesda, Maryland.

My last and first thank-you goes to you, Dear Husband, my helpmate, soulmate, beloved. My eternal, joyful thank you, Lord.

On Succor and Stitching: Thoughts Shared

A lifetime ago, the grandmother dream came to me. Up through my teenage years, my two grandmothers lived an hour or two away from us. Even now, more than half a century later, photos of both grandmothers sit in my living room. My children feel they know these women from the stories I tell. Both were courageous. I loved them dearly. They frequent my thoughts. I regarded Grandma, May Davina Ross Hamilton— my tall, stately, stern, devout Protestant paternal grandmother—with utmost respect, admiration, and love, touched with awe. I adored Nana, Eleanor Thora Ferris Patton Crowley—my elegant, dramatic, artistic, Catholic maternal grandmother. She is still the most fascinating woman I've ever known.

Eleanor Thora Ferris Patton Crowley

As a freshman, I sat chatting late of an evening in my college dorm, wearing red Dr. Denton pajamas with a red wool shawl wrapped around my shoulders for warmth. Smiling at my garb, a dorm-mate opined, "You'll make the perfect grandmother, Elly." Though ensconced in ivy's halls to focus on career, I loved that prediction. "A grandmother," my heart confirmed. "That's what I want to be."

Amply blessed and busy as a mother, I told myself, "I'll be better as a grandmother, for then I won't be pulled in so many directions." As I remembered it, Nana had *devoted* herself to me when I was a child.

In retrospect, I realize both my grandmothers were devoting themselves to me because I was visiting them or they me. That happy visiting time, of course, was but a respite from their busy lives. Busy lives in the modern mix often include lives lived great distances apart. As a grandmother now myself, I've happily discovered that I can visit with grand-children without the plane or the planning—by stitching, thinking the while of the precious child for whom I am sewing. As a grandmother, I can so immerse myself in the task, that it becomes an antidote for the loneliness—a meditation, a succor, a salve for the soul.

May Davina Ross Hamilton

My wish for you, Dear Reader, is that this book will bring you sweet stitching visits with someone you love. You and I understand that the love with which we stitch becomes part of the quilt as surely as does the thread. We can feel the soul of that love when we look at a carefully made old quilt. Others will sense our feelings, even when our hands are long stilled. Isn't it an uplifting thought—while our stitching comforts us now, our stitches themselves might comfort hearts yet unborn?

Preface

A Place to Begin

Baltimore Album Quilt: *n* A mid-nineteenth-century quilt presenting a collection of different (predominantly appliquéd, often symbolic) blocks in a gridded set, inscribed "Baltimore" or having a provenance authenticating its origin in or near Baltimore City, Maryland. Album quilts made in another time or place may be called Baltimore-style Albums.

Symbol: *n* Something that stands for or represents something else; a visible sign of something invisible (often an abstract idea).

Rush-hour traffic races and *parfum d'auto* hangs heavy on the air. It is deep July and bright-hot this early morning as I complete my walk to Barnes & Noble near my home in D.C., where I'll spend the day writing. Truth to tell, this commercial stretch of Jefferson Davis Highway has no pleasant vista. So on imagination's wing, I escape from the car dealerships and fast food places into the distant past. George Washington—whose turf this was—might have cantered along this path. My thoughts lift back to fair Virginia on the brink of our country's founding—and then edge closer to the mid 1840s to 1850s and veer east, to Maryland—to Baltimore, the city where our country's most famous quilts, the Baltimore Albums, first sprang to life.

Lost in thought, I contemplate those richly appliquéd Baltimore Album quilts, the antique style become so precious to me. *Baltimore Elegance* intends to teach their style through a pattern mode so easy, so accessible, that a stitcher will be inspired to fashion such a quilt even for a very young child, perhaps even *with* a young child (and so this book includes projects and paraphernalia for sewing with a child). This book is for all who dream of stitching an eyeful of beauty, bright colors, and happy memories: A "keeping quilt" to greet a loved one's waking moments and to blanket them— to protect them as cloud-cover shields against harsh sun—and to speak a fond "goodnight" and "happy day tomorrow."

If a quiltmaker is very, very lucky, her next quilt will be for a child. That child will grow up knowing both the stitcher and the love she stitched. The simple though eloquent Albums this book envisions are ones whose hand-wrought beauty so speaks to the soul, that though carefully used, they will be well-treated and survive to warm another generation.

A quilt made and used with love becomes a symbol. Symbols are potent transmitters of valuable information. The use of symbols was the great eye-opener for me as I began my Album journey at an exhibit one day: these quilts were using symbols to speak without words. With this discovery, I recognized the old Album quilts as letters to the present, telling us about the hopes and beliefs of the makers, and about the times and places in which they lived. To my early 1980s sensibilities, the style of these quilts was shockingly fresh and *bright*. In that era, we traditionalists relied on small calicoes and subdued color to evoke the patina of an old quilt. By contrast, these large (up to 131″ square) Albums hailed one's attention!

Baltimores have earned the title "classic." You and I define classic as something that sets a standard for all time. We feel a greatness and a magic in the presence of something humanly made, superbly done. The complex beauty of the Baltimore touched me. I would come to feel that these Album-bound blocks were like pages in a poetry or history book: meaning-filled documents begging further understanding. As a young mother, overspent, I felt those first-seen Albums spoke to my soul. At day's end, I stopped silently before one quilt and stared at its center block: a wheel of hearts, appliquéd from a single layer of fabric. I was mesmerized! Like Alice falling into Wonderland, I felt myself pulled through the block's open-circle center and into a fascination that holds me still.

It takes time for love to blossom. Returning from the exhibition, my Album courtship began. It began in a young mom's time—time stolen from the night. I sat up late drawing Baltimore blocks into appliqué patterns. I was struck by how often certain motifs were repeated—not the whole pattern, but the motifs. First it was the acorn that struck me as significant... and puzzling. Acorns occurred in flowerpots or cornucopias—places where in real life we'd want to remove them! I pursued the symbolism of acorns in an old *Language of the Flowers:* Acorns stand for longevity, while the oak tree itself stands for strength against adversity. What happy wishes to stitch into a quilt! The more I studied these quilts and the more I stitched their blocks, the more I suspected intentional symbolism.

As I worked on the old quilts, I felt the mystery of my connectedness to others. Not literally—in the sense of held hands or shared conversations—but spiritually, in a shared understanding of our very humanity, of our brief time here on this earth. To my joy, others were intrigued by the Albums and joined this journey. Their enthusiasm encouraged me to delve deeper into these quilts, to research how they were made and by whom. Because my fellow Album-makers swelled so in numbers, this era—now in its third decade—has been widely dubbed the "Baltimore Album Revival." During this time, I have studied and stitched intensively and written numerous appliqué books. I wrote and stitched from being a mother of young children on into being a grandmother.

Making History in Our Everyday Lives

It is hard to think of ourselves as making history in our everyday lives…but we do. Future ages will look back on us and know important things about us through our quilts, and so what our quilts bear witness to matters. As quiltmakers ourselves, we know something of the character it takes to envision a whole—and the diligence needed to stitch that vision on to its finish as a quilt. We also know something of hand appliqué's effect upon the stitcher herself. Appliquérs speak of their stitching with something akin to reverence. So, of course, recent scientific data pleased us as it affirmed that stitching reduces stress and lowers blood pressure. Appliqué focuses the mind and salves the soul. The longer one stays on that journey—going into herself for inspiration and out again to listen to what the design wants to become—the longer she stitches, the more something new evolves within her. This care of the soul through stitching is no new idea. Listen to advice stitched on an antique sampler:

While you, my dear, your needlework attend
Observe the counsel of a faithful friend
And strive an inward ornament to gain
Or all your needlework shall prove in vain.

What one gift from the old Albums might we single out? To me, it is that they bear witness to the spirit in which a person plays out the hand she's dealt: the Album makers' troubles were surely no less than our own, yet they left us such gifts of beauty! In *The Pursuit of Excellence*, Charles Murray writes, "Ask yourself: What sculpture, novel, or painting…produced *since* 1950 will *still* be considered important two hundred years from now?" His theory is that great accomplishment in the arts has been fostered by transcendent goals like Truth and Goodness. "Without these high goals," he suggests, "art can rise to the highest rungs of craft, captivating entertainments can be produced. But in the same way that a goldsmith needs gold, a culture needs a coherent sense of the transcendent to foster great accomplishment."

Some say we live in a secular age. Yet who can survey our quilts and not ask, "Will the future not find at least some of this work worth labeling 'classic'?" And does a search for the transcendent have something to do with it? Listen, a moment, to some brief answers inscribed on the old Albums. Judge whether they do indeed convey a Reach for the Good, the True, and the Beautiful:

- *May you, my child, in Virtue's path proceed. / Her ways are pleasant and to Heaven lead. / Then when you leave this tenement of clay / Angels shall guide you to the realm of day.*

Or,

- *To General Taylor of the Rio Grande, From your Rough and Ready. E Pluribus Unum*

And another message:

- *Let all inspired with Godly mirth / Sing solemn hymns of Praise. —inscribed March, 1844*

The most common inscription is some version of Remember me:

- *Should I be parted far from thee / Look at this and think of me.*

And on another quilt, a reply:

- *I'll remember dear Angie, whatever betide / I'll remember you always / Tho waters…divide.*

What message will *our* quilts leave to the future? All the quilters I have known have been quietly courageous. They've met life with grace. The old Albums' message is faith, hope, and love. Many of our own quilts echo that. Surely our own perseverance must also shine through.

People argue that we are a culture with no common transcendent purpose—that increasingly, we may not even *have* a common culture. I'm not sure this is true. Even before 9/11, today's quilters protected their unity. Have you noticed that at a quilt conference, no one ever asks, "What kind of work do you do?" They know what you do that's important: you quilt. Without giving it much thought, quilters stitch clear of dissension. It is as though we have an unwritten rule: to concentrate on the things that unite us and avoid things that divide us. I love Show and Tell, for there this gentle unity becomes apparent. As we show a quilt, for a brief moment, the audience tries to see the world as we do and supports us with applause.

Old quilts bear witness to wisdom. They give us comfort and courage in our time of need. They give us such joy! This art, the old *and* the new, helps explain us to ourselves; it ties past to present and us to the future. Both the old ones and the new ones bear witness to lives that accept and rejoice in the day, which the Lord hath made. We're told we're spoiled here in this land of milk and honey. But I've heard no spoiled whining in our appliqué classes. All I've heard are needles singing a joyful chorus. The voices in our Albums are aunts and mothers, daughters and sisters, grandmothers and wives. They speak their love through their quilts. They will continue to speak when the hand that made them is stilled. This honorable sisterhood welcomes you, dear reader!

Back to the Present: Visible Signs of Invisible Things

I feel the need to make simpler Albums these days, for I am a grandmother of very young grandchildren and I have come to believe in the power of symbols. My soul smiles when a young mother says in my class, "I'm making this (this heirloom Album, this legacy) for my son; he is seven." For young mothers, I believe, the time to start such things is early. So too, for grand mothers, the time to begin is early, for the ability to continue stitching is a longed-for blessing, not a certainty.

Today as I walk to that bookstore I call "my office," I plan to begin this Preface and I'm trying to put myself into a conducive mood. The Preface is my favorite part of a book to write, but also the most difficult, wrested, as so much of it is, from the imagination. I spot on my left the tentative outlines of a path. It heads up a steep hillside. Although a high, dense privet hedge comes between my view and the direction of Barnes & Noble a mile or so away, I believe I can reach my destination from here. This is just what I need—a touch of country amidst this urban rush hour! And so, pulled to the peace of a more bucolic route, I leave the highway and venture up this little-traveled path.

The difference underfoot is immediate! I can feel the ground rising beneath my feet. My spirit is climbing, too, for higher up the hill the street noise stills, the air smells freshly field-like, the grasses have grown tall. Summer green and willowy, wildflower colors sparkle against the grasses: dandelion yellows and bachelor's button blues, Indian paintbrush oranges and…Suddenly a gentle wind wraps round me, caresses my bare forearms like a cool damp shawl, tickles my unclothed calves. Queen Ann's Lace blooms—white blossom-crowded caps—are being teased by my visiting breeze. For just a moment they dance gaily, bobbing to an unseen rhythm.

Cheering to witness, this motion is a visible sign of invisible air currents. I think of the symbols in the Albums—the visible signs of invisible things. The ladies who made those quilts were so attuned to symbols: they, with their Language of the Flowers; they, with their sense of the here and the hereafter; they, so conscious of God's close presence. Is the wind itself a symbol of something unseen? The Albums have made me wonder, have made me want to believe not simply in the physical fact of air currents, but in the mystical possibilities beyond scientific explanation. I can see the floral dance, can feel the breeze. I cannot see the wind, but I see its effect, know its presence.

Through symbols, visible signs of invisible things, old Baltimore's needlewomen spoke ancient tongues, quite comprehensible even now. I decide that I will note Baltimore's symbolism on this new book's block patterns. The possibilities of symbolism dance through my imagination as I scan my small city hilltop. Butterflies flutter nearby: are they not visible signs of invisible things? Bees (in Album symbol-speak, "a sign of industry") buzz; last autumn's seed pods ("fertility") lie beneath a wild hibiscus, silently marking the passage of time; wild blackberries ("fruitfulness," "the blessings of this earth") are quickening to ripeness as I pass. Birds (a bluebird for "life of the soul") call and answer each other. I strain to see them, want to know them: there is a mockingbird, then a catbird, a female cardinal…and now a downy feather flutters toward my path.

As I climb a bit higher, I am on what I can now see is a large berm. There is little topsoil over the gravel and the broad swath I've just traversed is fairly bare. Yet growth is accumulating, and its exuberant variety has lifted my spirit. This morning walk has been full of visible signs of invisible things! Excited about the book, a chance to write once again on the beloved Album quilts, I quicken my step. I'm filled now, as so often, with gratitude. As silent as the gentle breeze, my thoughts whisper, "Thank you."

And thank you, my fellow quiltmaker. Thank you for contemplating joining this old and honorable sisterhood—the Album-makers. May you be inspired to stitch a simpler Album. Its beauty may well lift even hearts yet unborn!

Elly Sienkiewicz

Arlington, Virginia, July 14, 2003

Getting Started

Getting Started does just that. It presents an understanding of Baltimore Album quilts and their design, followed by a handbook of appliqué basics. The Oak Leaf and Reel Pattern (also taught in Lesson 1) illustrates the first techniques, serving as a preview of the journey ahead! The lessons are progressive: each builds upon the previous one. Lesson 1 assumes (perhaps wrongly) that you are a novice; Lesson 2 presumes that you've learned the skills taught in Lesson 1—and so on up to Lesson 6. With this approach, even the most experienced appliquérs will learn something they did not know before. Between Lessons 1 and 6 lie all manner of wonders—from basic one-layer appliqué; on to perfect stems and circles; to Layered, Dimensional, Ultrasuede, and Ribbon Appliqué; then on to embellishments, including inked, beaded, and embroidered.

A Note on Handedness

With admiration for the adaptable lefties among us, this book instructs from a right-handed perspective.

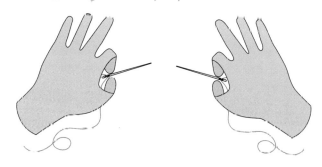

What Creates the Classic Look?

Album quilts (like photo, record, or stamp albums) house a collection on a theme. These collections of different blocks set in a grid invite the collector to make choices all along the way, beginning with the fabric. Classic Baltimore Album quilts contain high color contrast. The backgrounds (the ground upon which the appliqué is stitched) are typically white or off-white, while the appliqués themselves run boldly from white (light) to black (dark). When they talk about us in 150 years, they'll note that we twenty-first-century Album-makers used as many printed backgrounds as plain ones, we chose backgrounds that reflect all tints and shades, and sometimes we even made a patchwork of different background fabrics. We're blessed to live in freedom. Enjoy this freedom in your quiltmaking. The final word on fabric choice? Your way is the best way!

Airiness

Airiness is a common element of classic Album quilts. For example, lots of background fabric appears behind the appliqués. Even in our small, simplified *Baltimore Elegance* patterns, the gesture is one of airiness. Flowers are lifted so that light (background) moves around and between them. It is fun to look at such blocks in the fanciest old Baltimores and see that there are usually unrealistically few (or no) stems descending from a lush cluster of flowers (see Reproduction Pattern 8, Urn of Flowers, on page 157). Certain Album blocks excel at realism, but it seems that airiness trumps realism. After so long in the company of these old Albums, you might think the quilters sometimes tried to show unseen things, such as a breeze, a beam of sunlight, or the unseen hand of God.

Block Subject Matter

The subject matter of Album blocks is diverse and often symbolic. Some favorite motifs (fleurs-de-lis, eagles, doves, wreaths of grape and laurel) have familiar symbolic meanings. Symbols were a common tongue in that era. Although the written word is the most specific of all symbols, compulsory public education was just coming onto the scene in the Album era. So that you can enjoy some of our blocks on this level, symbolic meanings have been noted for patterns wherever possible. And because sweet sayings, quotes, and poems were inscribed on many Album blocks, inscriptions from antique quilts and samplers appear throughout this book. The combined impact of the prettiness of the appliqués, the silent witness of the symbols, and the eloquence of the inscriptions is one of beneficence. And, of course, beauty—both of aspect and of spirit—is what we want in our own Album quilt. We want it to wrap with warmth and love; to comfort from behind the veil of time.

Classic Colors

The *staple appliqué colors* in the classic Albums are Turkey red and Victoria green. History is part of the romance of the Albums, and history is in these colors. Colorfast red fabric originated in the Middle East. But even after its manufacture in the West began, the name "Turkey red" held. And Victoria? The decorative arts of an entire era are named after the world's most influential queen. And so is the favorite green—"Victoria green," which is a yellowy split-pea green.

But what did Turkey red and Victoria green really look like? It's worth a look at antique quilts of the Baltimore era (mid-1840s to mid-1850s) or at their pictures in *Baltimore Beauties and Beyond: Volume I* (Quilts 1–4). You'll see this famous red/green couple amid the classic full-color palette of the Albums. These quilts were high contrast and showy! The Baltimore Album Revival, now in its third decade, flashes marvelous "beyond" Baltimore blocks, sets, and color schemes.

Visual texture seasons the classic look. The most vivacious antique Baltimores dance with prints and plains. Prints include elegant florals, geometrics (plaids, checks, and stripes), conversation prints (interlocked chains were a favorite), and watermark-like moiré designs. Ombré prints (prints with increasing, then decreasing saturations of color) characterize the most sophisticated antebellum Baltimores. Prints evocative of old Baltimore are being reproduced today in my designer lines by Robert Kaufman Fabrics. By nature, Baltimore-style Albums are dramatic and enticing. Exciting fabric use pulls the observer to study an Album up close, thereby appreciating the quiltmaker's exuberance afresh.

Number of Blocks

The number of blocks has a striking effect on the visual impact of the quilt. An odd number of blocks, rather than an even number, gives a strong visual focus to a quilt because there is always a central focal point. One block enlarged into a center medallion, or the same block repeated four times, also provides a strong center. The repetition of similar blocks (wreaths or crossed sprays, for example) can give an Album quilt a coherent design.

Jen's Baby Baltimore, 40½″ × 40½″, by Joyce A. Barone
Odd number of blocks gives strong central focus to quilt
(see page 40 for larger view).

Quiet Moments, 36½″ × 41½″, by Bette F. Augustine
Repeated blocks form center medallion
(see page 41 for larger view).

Sweet Samantha, 36″ × 54″, by Donna Hall Bailey
Repeating one block gives design appealing strength
(see page 35 for larger view).

Sashing and Borders

Sashing frames the blocks, a border frames the quilt. Both can unify a quilt. Look at the needleartist quilts in this book and notice how sashing and border use differs!

The borders in antique Baltimores are usually smaller—one-half to two-thirds the width of one block. Often the borders in turn-of-the-twenty-first-century Baltimore-style Albums are almost as wide as a block.

Basic Baltimore: Angel to Come, 42″ × 34″, by Karen A. Evans
See how effective even the simplest wholecloth border can be
(see page 40 for a larger view).

Design Your Classic

This book explores elegant, easy appliqué; the step-by-step instruction on finishing your blocks into a quilt is best left to a basic quiltmaking book (see Courses and Sources on page 173). As you begin, however, think about the practical questions: How many blocks do you want your quilt to have? How wide do you want the border to be? As you look at the quilts pictured throughout this book, think about how you would set your finished Album blocks. Think about what gives an Album—this collection of squares—its cohesion.

The quilts of contributing needleartists grace this book's pages. The block patterns and border motifs are provided in the pattern section (pages 121–172). You could copy one of those sets and borders, or you could design your own Album quilt.

- Some quiltmakers stitch blocks for a while, then pin a combination of quilt blocks, fabric mock-ups, and patterns (roughly colored in) on a design wall.
- Other quiltmakers snap a picture of their blocks and arrange those photo-blocks in different layouts.
- Still others work on graph paper and arrange the 1″ pattern miniatures on each pattern page in experimental sets. These colorless images emphasize the pull of airiness and empty space.

As you stitch, the quilt concepts will come!

What You'll Need

Tools and Notions

CUTTING

Scissors

5″ fabric scissors (which cut to the point) for cutting appliqué shapes

3″ embroidery scissors for cutting into corners or turning under points

8″ sewing shears for the traditional cutting of blocks, sashings, and borders

5″ paper scissors for cutting templates

5″ scissors (strong) for cutting stacked paper, such as multiple templates or Papercut Appliqué designs (Tailor-point Gingher scissors G5C are the best I have found for finely cutting through up to eight layers of freezer paper.)

Rotary cutter, Plexiglas ruler, cutting mat (optional) for cutting the blocks, borders, and sashing

PINS, NEEDLES, AND THREAD

Pins

Fine ball-headed ³⁄₄″ **pins** for appliqué

1¹⁄₂″ silk pins or **small gold safety pins** for holding the appliqué fabric square to the background

Needles

Sharps needles size #10 or #11 are the traditional needles for prepared appliqué, where the seam has already been turned under (pages 18–20). These needles can be used for all the lessons.

Milliner's needles size #10 or #11 are ideal for Nonprepared Appliqué. These slightly longer needles facilitate the sweeping under that is required for needleturn. They are sometimes called *milliner's straw needles* (for sewing flowers on straw hats) or simply *straw needles*. These needles can be used for Lesson 1 and for all appliqué.

Crewel or embroidery needles size #9 or #10 for one or two strands of embroidery floss

Chenille size #24 for up to three strands of embroidery floss

Chenille size #22 for basic silk-ribbon embroidery

Note The larger the number size of the needle, the smaller the needle's diameter and its eye. Thus a size #12 needle is a finer needle than a size #8.

Thread

Use a fine thread in a neutral color or in a color matched to the appliqué, not to the background fabric. I recommend YLI's Silk 100 thread or Mettler 60-weight cotton thread. YLI carries Elly Sienkiewicz designer thread sets, including one *Baltimore Album Set* of reds and greens and one *Appliqué Traveler's Set* to finish the colors you need—including my favorite neutral color, #235—for traveling.

MARKING AND MEASURING

Dark and light fabric marking pens

Fine mechanical pencil

Pigma .01 pen for inscribing blocks

Silver Sakura Gelly Roll Pen for tracing around templates. It marks both light and dark fabrics.

³/₄″-wide masking tape

Repositionable clear tape

12″–18″ gridded ruler

Freezer paper

8¹/₂″ square gridded ruler (see Sources and Courses on page 173) **OR**

Template plastic Make an opaque 8¹/₂″ × 8¹/₂″ square of template plastic with centering lines for trimming the finished blocks.

Each pattern design image fits within a 7″ × 7″ square. An 8¹/₂″ square template makes an 8″ × 8″ finished square when a ¹/₄″ seam allowance is used for piecing, allowing space around each pattern design.

To easily center the stitched design, use a permanent pen to mark vertical, horizontal, and diagonal center lines on the template.

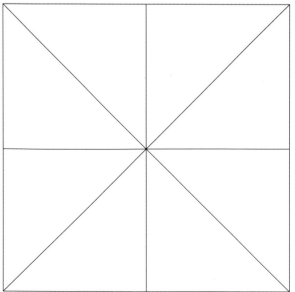

Make 8¹/₂″ square opaque plastic template marked with vertical, horizontal, and diagonal centers.

PATTERN TRANSFER

Lightbox for tracing patterns (see page 119)

Freezer paper for templates and papercuts (see pages 114–117)

Clear transparency sheets, PatternEase pattern transfer product by Pellon, or **Quilter's Vinyl** for Pattern Transfer Method 5: Pattern Veil (see pages 118–119)

BASTING

Clover appliqué pins

Gluestick

Roxanne's GLUE-BASTE-IT

PRESSING

Iron (with a linen setting)

Breadboard or other hard ironing surface

Magic Sizing spray finish

Paper towels (without heavy embossing) as pressing cloths

Worn terry-cloth towel

EMBELLISHING

6-Strand DMC Embroidery Floss: colors as needed for embellishment

Seed beads: colors as needed for embellishment

Shaded wired ribbon: widths and colors as needed for Dimensional Appliqué (see Courses and Sources on page 173)

OPTIONAL

Sewing light and magnification for hand work

Thimble for appliqué and hand piecing

Fabric

The exact amount of fabric you'll need depends on many factors, including the number of blocks, whether you use sashing, and the width of your borders. The following rough guidelines give you some idea of the fabric you'll need. Figure the yardage for your quilt based on your particulars. *Prewashing all fabric is wise.*

APPLIQUÉ

Scraps or fat quarters are needed for the appliquéd colors. Green and a floral color (traditionally red) dominate Album appliqué, so stock up on ¹/₂ to full yards of your favorites.

BACKGROUND

The appliqués are stitched to a background fabric. Before you start a *Baltimore Elegance* quilt, estimate the yardage of background needed for the whole top. These Baltimores can contain from 4 blocks up to 25 or more—plan on at least 9″ × 9″ of background fabric for each block. For blocks with the same background, ⅜ yard of fabric is plenty for a 4-block quilt. For a 25-block quilt with the same background, you should have about 1½ yards of background fabric. If you want to vary the background, buy a combination of fabrics. Always consider buying extra to allow your muses free reign.

SASHING AND BORDERS

The fabric required for sashing and borders depends on the number of blocks and the way you plan to set them together.

Sashings are usually 1½″ to 2½″ wide. For a 4-block quilt, you'll need about ⅛ yard of fabric. For a 25-block quilt, you'll need about ⅝ yard of fabric.

Borders are usually 4½″ to 9½″ wide and can be cut on the lengthwise or crosswise grain. If you cut the borders on the crosswise grain, you'll need to piece them for a larger quilt. If you cut them on the lengthwise grain, you'll have fabric left over. As with many decisions in quilting, the choice is yours.

For a small 4-block quilt with 4½″ borders, you'll need about ⅝ yard of fabric (cut crosswise). For a larger 25-block quilt with 9½″ borders, you'll need about 2 yards of fabric.

BACKING

Depending on the size of your finished quilt, you'll need about a yard of fabric for a small (4-block) quilt and up to 4⅛ yards for a larger (25-block) quilt. For larger quilts, extra wide background fabrics are available, so you don't have to piece the backing.

There are two Elly Sienkiewicz signature lines for Robert Kaufman Fabrics. *Beyond Baltimore* is my appliqué theme line; the Spoken Without a Word collection contains prints, solids, and extra-wide (110″) backings.

BATTING

For an antique look, use a very thin batting. The thinnest batting made today is Hobbs Thermore, a polyester material. The three thinnest cotton battings are Hobbs Heirloom Organic 100% Cotton, Heirloom Organic Cotton With Scrim, and Heirloom Bleached 100% Cotton. With a pale appliqué background and a thin batting, you need a pale backing fabric so that it does not show through to the quilt top.

The Happiness Is In the Journey!

To begin your journey, skim the following appliqué basics to learn these techniques:

- The tack stitch—the basic appliqué stitch
- Prepared and Nonprepared Appliqué—the two basic families of appliqué

Take a minute to peruse the pattern section (starting on page 114), which explains pattern transfer and offers small block and border patterns. For those already working on larger (12½″–16″ design image) Baltimore blocks, eight elaborate Album block patterns, which you will need to enlarge, conclude the patterns.

From there, proceed to the lessons; then to Courses and Sources.

In the lessons, you will need to refer to Pattern Transfer Methods (starting on page 115) and Appliqué Basics (starting on the next page) until the methods become second nature to you. By the end of the lessons, you'll have gained expertise and confidence, so that your most elegant appliqué dreams can come true.

For those of you lucky enough to have a little girl to stitch with, the projects include both adult and child versions of sewing aprons, sewing cases, totes with a Babushka pincushion doll, simple neck pockets as a child's first hand-sewing project, and pillowcases as a child's gift or a machine-work lesson for later. For Babushka (Russian for "old lady" or "grandma") herself, the last project is a block carrying case to store your works in progress…because, for Album-makers, happiness is in the journey!

*May this year's roses be
Many and sweet
And few be the thorns
Where wander thy feet.*

Appliqué *n A patch of fabric (usually decorative) sewn down to a background fabric*

Appliqué *vt To apply one fabric on top of another; the stitching of a decorative patch of fabric to a background fabric*

Cutaway Appliqué *n A nonprepared appliqué method in which the seam allowance of the appliqué motif is cut out of a larger piece of fabric, a little bit at a time, just before the seam is needleturned under and stitched down*

Needleturn *vt To use a needle to turn under the appliqué seam, then tack stitch that seam fold in place to create points, curves, straight edges, and inside corners*

Nonprepared Appliqué *n An appliqué in which the needle is used to turn under the seam allowance a little bit at a time, just ahead of stitching; the process is turn and stitch, turn and stitch*

Prepared Appliqué *n An appliqué in which the seam allowance is turned under and held in place all around (basted, glued, or melded to freezer paper) before stitching begins*

Tack stitch *n The most common stitch for appliqué with a turned seam allowance, sometimes called the appliqué stitch; used for both Prepared Appliqué and Nonprepared Appliqué*

Thread *n A fine continuous strand used to sew fabric*

Threading the Needle

Pinch freshly cut thread end.

Rather than push the thread through the eye of the needle (thread the needle), I find it easiest to move the eye of the needle over the thread (needle the thread).

Cut a 20″ length of thread. Pinch the freshly cut thread end, allowing $\frac{1}{16}$″ or so to stick up between your left thumb and forefinger.

With your right hand, move the eye of the needle over and down onto the thread. When the thread peeks above the eye, grab it and pull through a 5″ length.

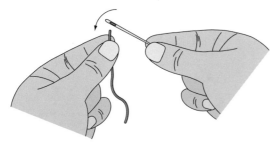

Move eye of needle over and down onto thread.

Basting

Baste *vt To temporarily attach one fabric to another in preparation for sewing it in place with finer stitches*

Pin-Basting

Use straight pins to pin the appliqué to the background. The small $\frac{3}{4}$″-long ball-headed pins (often called appliqué pins) work best. The ball head makes these pins easy to handle even for the very mature appliquér. Their short length prevents thread from catching on them as you stitch. Always use more than one pin so the appliqué doesn't shift or pivot. *Caution:* Even modern pins can leave rust spots over time.

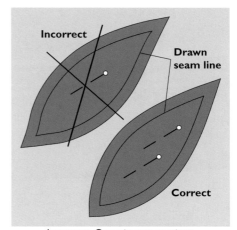

Incorrect: One pin acts as pivot.
Correct: More than one pin holds appliqué stable.

Stitch-Basting

This is what is traditionally meant by basting: Use a milliner's needle [a], nonslippery thread, and medium-length ($\frac{1}{8}$″–$\frac{1}{4}$″) running stitches [b]. Use appliqué pins [c] to hold each piece in place while you baste. Begin with a knot [d]. Secure the stitches before ending and remove the stitches after you have appliquéd with finer stitches.

Stitch-basting

Glue-Basting With a Gluestick

I avoid putting gluestick on the wrong side of the finished appliqué because I am concerned about migration or staining. Instead I apply the glue on the seam allowance or on a freezer-paper template (to be used inside the appliqué) that will be removed. Gluestick has an advantage over the more liquid white glue in that it adheres immediately. However, once dried, it takes less of the white glue to hold fabric tightly to fabric.

To attach fabric to fabric: Use a gluestick to apply a dab of glue to hold the point in the Freezer Paper Inside technique (see pages 18–20).

To attach freezer paper to fabric: In appliqués prepared with Freezer Paper Inside, dab gluestick on the exposed back of the freezer paper to baste the appliqué to the background fabric. Lesson 1 (page 54) suggests using gluestick instead of an iron to hold the turned-under seam allowance to the paper. The secret is that the shiny side of the paper will hold the glued fabric long enough to do the appliqué. But twisting the paper/fabric adhesion breaks the seal, allowing the paper to be easily removed from inside the appliqué.

A gluestick is particularly helpful when doing miniature work.

Freezer paper, shiny side up

Gluestick dabbed on the exposed seam

Dab gluestick along back of exposed seam allowance. Gluestick on seam allowance will be pressed to background fabric.

Finger-press appliqué in place, and it's ready to stitch.

Glue-Basting With White Glue

We all have our own level of acceptable risk. I don't yet use this glue-basting method because the glue goes underneath the finished surface of the appliqué. However, I am beginning to listen to its siren song! Put a tiny dot (a pinprick) of diluted white glue on the wrong side of the appliqué, ½˝ in from the turn line, giving the seam allowance room to turn under. The droplets are so minuscule that they do not bleed through to the right side of the fabric. Dot at the same interval you would pin. Roxanne's GLUE-BASTE-IT conveniently packages this glue with a hypodermic needle cap to dispense tiny drops. It comes

in a smaller travel size as well. Washing is suggested to remove the glue. Quilting aficionadas store the glue with a long ball-headed quilter's pin in the hypodermic dispenser to keep it from getting clogged.

After appliqué is complete, tiny dots on wrong side of white-glue–basted bird are not visible and could, if desired, be washed out.

Heat-Basting

Use the hot tip of an iron to meld freezer paper to the wrong side of fabric in pin-basting-like intervals. Heat-baste to smoothly fold the fabric into a curved edge. Or heat-baste an appliqué to the background fabric using Freezer Paper Inside. The still-exposed shiny side of the freezer paper beneath the appliqué makes this possible. Set the iron to cotton. A too-hot iron setting, such as linen, may scorch the background fabric.

Knots

Quilter's Knot

For cotton thread, a spit knot works fine. For silk thread, however, the knot affectionately known as the quilter's knot works best. Once you learn it, it's hard to go back! Tie this knot in the end farthest from the eye of the needle.

Pinch the thread tail over the shank of the needle, holding it between your right thumb and forefinger.

Tail of thread

Needle shank

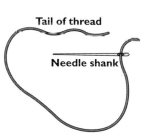

Hold thread tail over shank of needle.

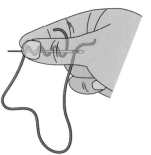

Wrap thread around needle.

With your left hand, wrap the thread around the needle (4 wraps for cotton, 10 wraps for silk), then scootch your right hand forward so your pinch catches those wraps too.

Keep pinching. With your left hand, pull the needle all the way through the thread wraps until only the knotted tail remains behind, pinched between your right thumb and forefinger. This makes a tidy French knot, also known as a quilter's knot, on the thread tail.

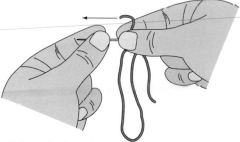

Pull needle through thread wraps to make French knot, also known as quilter's knot.

Beginning Appliqué: Hiding the Knot

You can hide the knotted thread tail by slipping it into the seam from the top as you begin, or you can leave it on the back of the block.

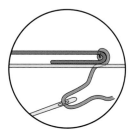

Hide tail in seam.

If you are using 100-weight silk thread, the back of the block may be the best place to leave the knot. Even with ten twists around the needle, this superfine thread can pop through one layer of fabric. It is less likely to pop through two layers. Tradition tells us that the back of the block should look as good as the front. Consider, though, that one can think of a knot left on the back as an act of faith—faith that the block will be finished!

Leave knot on back of block.

Knotting the Thread at the Eye of the Needle

Imagine this scenario: You are using cotton thread and have just two more stitches to finish, but the thread is so short that it is falling out of the needle. Try this knot. If you are using

oh-so-slippery silk thread, you must tie it at the eye of the needle to keep it from slipping out of the needle as you sew. Simply tie a square knot at the eye of the needle. This very secure knot is almost like tying your shoes!

1. Tie the right thread over the left. Pull the tie tightly to the eye of the needle.

Thread goes right over left.

2. Tie again, with the left thread in your right hand, so that you are tying right over left again.

Thread goes right over left again.

3. The secret is to pull the tie back tightly against the eye of the needle, just like you pull your shoelace back tightly against your sneaker. If the knot loosens, simply pull the thread ends so the knot slides back tightly against the eye.

Pull tightly against eye.

Knotless Start for Embellishment

Entering from the right side of the fabric allows you to begin your first embroidery stitch (a chain stitch, for example) from the top.

1. Fold a single 36″-long single strand of floss in half. Thread the folded floss through the eye of the needle.

Thread needle with folded floss.

2. Push the needle down through the top (right side) of the fabric. Leave the loop on top of the fabric [a].

3. Push the needle up from the bottom and pass the needle through the loop on top of the fabric. Pull taut so the tiny slip knot rests on the fabric.

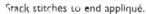

Pass needle up through loop.

 *Note* For a stitch that begins on the wrong side of the fabric (such as a French knot), push the needle up from underneath, leaving the loop on the bottom. Then push the needle down from the top, passing through the loop. You are now ready to begin the French knot by pushing up again from the bottom.

Mending Appliqué Stitches

Broken thread? Thread knotted midseam? Cut the thread at the knot and start again.

1. Pull the cut thread to the wrong side of the appliqué, leaving a ½″ tail [a]. (If necessary, pull out a couple of stitches to leave this tail.)

2. Re-thread your needle, knot the tail [b], and resume appliquéing ¾″ before the broken thread. If you are sewing with slippery silk, pierce a couple of the original stitches as you stitch over them. This will keep the repaired stitches from loosening.

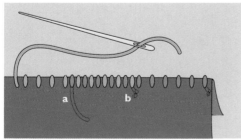

Overlapped stitches on right side of fabric

Did an unwanted knot require this repair? Traditionally beeswax was used to keep thread from knotting. Thread Heaven is a modern product that serves the same purpose magically well.

Ending Appliqué Stitches

Stacked Stitches

Taking three tiny stitches on top of each other [a] beneath an appliqué on the wrong side of the background is a time-honored way to secure your final stitches.

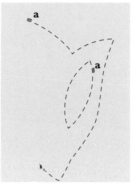

Stack stitches to end appliqué.

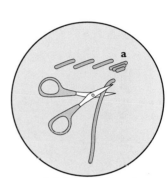

Sink finishing thread between the layers.

French Knot

If you're stitching with silk, the French knot finish that follows will hold the thread best. This tidy finish excels with cotton thread as well.

Put the needle through to the back of the block. Slip the needle under that last stitch [a] and wrap the tail three times around the needle. Pinch these wraps and pull the needle through. Sink the thread and clip the tail [b].

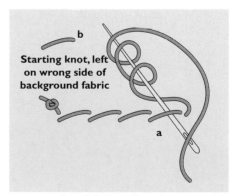

Starting knot, left on wrong side of background fabric

French knot ends appliqué.

Tack Stitch

Although the blanket, running, ladder, or blind stitch can appliqué, the only one you really need to know is the tack stitch. If you're curious, my *Appliqué 12 Easy Ways* explores those other stitches. Here, though, let's celebrate the tack stitch and refine it. The tack stitch holds all three layers—background, seam allowance, and appliqué—but shows only a tiny bit (the width of one needle) at the turn line.

1. Begin the tack stitch by pushing the needle up from underneath the background to emerge a full needle-width inside the fold of the appliqué [a]. When the needle emerges, pull the thread away from yourself until it is stopped by the knot on the back [b].

Push needle up from
back. Pull thread away.

2. Reinsert the point of the needle under the fold, as though you were putting it back into the same hole from which it emerged. The thread should not pull forward on the diagonal like a whipstitch, nor should it pull backward on the diagonal like a backstitch. What Goldilocks would call "just right" is a tiny, straight, perpendicular stitch 1 needle-width from the fold of the turned-under appliqué and then wrapping around the fold.

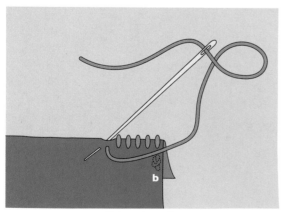

Reinsert needle.

3. To complete the stitch, exit the background fabric, scraping your finger beneath the block to make sure you're all the way through. All in one motion, turn the needle sharply upward again. Pierce up through the background, through the seam allowance, and through the appliqué, catching it just to the left of the previous stitch. Continue at a pace of about 10 stitches per inch. There is no "right" number of stitches per inch. The test is: Does the appliqué look good from the top, and does it hold well?

Prepared Appliqué With Freezer Paper Inside

There are two major appliqué families: the Prepared Appliqué family and the Nonprepared Appliqué family (starting on page 22). Of all the many ways to prepare appliqué, my favorite is to preturn and hold under the seam allowance using Freezer Paper Inside. With this technique, you iron the seam allowance to the shiny side of the freezer paper.

A Leaf's Lesson: Points and Curved Edges

Let this leaf and heart motif show you how to prepare (to preturn under) the seam allowance at outside corners, inside corners, straight edges, and curves using Freezer Paper Inside.

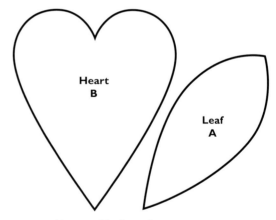

Heart and leaf template patterns

POINTS

1. Trace the leaf shape (Template A) onto freezer paper. Cut directly on the drawn line (adding no seam allowance). Pin it shiny side up to the wrong side of the appliqué fabric, on the bias where possible.

2. Cut out the leaf with a 3/16″ seam allowance beyond the freezer paper.

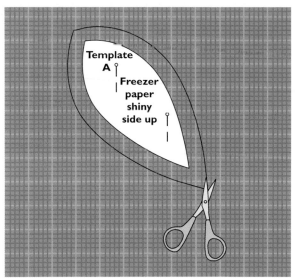

Pin freezer-paper template shiny side up on wrong side of fabric. Cut out with ³⁄₁₆″ seam allowance.

3. Pin the point of the freezer paper to a cardboard work surface so that it does not fold back as you iron [a]. Iron the seam allowance point perpendicular to the leaf [b].

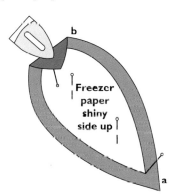

Pin point and iron seam allowance.

4. Smear gluestick across the width of the point [c]. Finger-press the left side and then the right into the glue so that the point is prepared (that is, it is all turned under). Heat-press the point once more to dry the glue. On an ovate leaf, do one point, then the other.

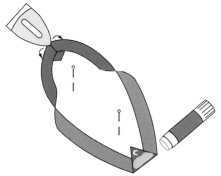

Finger-press sides of point into glue and press with an iron.

CURVES AND STRAIGHT EDGES

Curves or straight edges? Heat-baste the seam allowance with the point of the iron [a], spacing the intervals to keep the fabric turning in the desired direction. Finish the appliqué preparation by using a smoothing motion [b] with the side of the iron (like frosting a cake) to smoothly turn under the heat-basted sides. Remove the pins. From the front side, the appliqué should look finished.

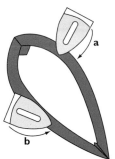

Fold sides of curves and straight edges and press.

Matters of the Heart: Outside and Inside Corners

1. Turn the outside point of a heart [d] first, as you did for the leaf.
2. Cut, dividing the seam allowance equally between the shoulders of the heart, stopping 3 needle-widths short of the paper [e]. *Hint:* Never clip right to the paper when using a freezer-paper template. If you think your clip has gone too far, clip the paper itself to allow a deeper stitch into the fabric corner.

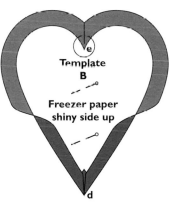

Cut between shoulders of heart.

3. Fold down half of the V-cut so that you can more easily access the opposite side.

Fold shoulder down to make
preparing inside corner easier.

4. When you've ironed one side, open it, then repeat the folding and ironing process for the opposite side.

Repeat on other side of heart.

5. When the heart is fully prepared over paper, pin or baste it to the background and appliqué it down.

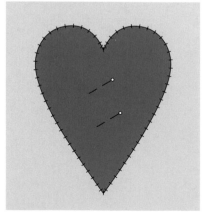

Appliqué prepared heart to background.

6. When you have finished all the stitching, remove the template by slitting the background fabric beneath the appliqué. Stop the cut ¼″ short of the appliquéd seamline. Pinch the seam between your thumb and forefinger to hold it steady and avoid stretching the stitches. Reach into the slit with tweezers or a hemostat and remove the freezer paper. Alternatively, you can leave an opening in the appliqué and remove the paper from the front, then complete the appliqué,

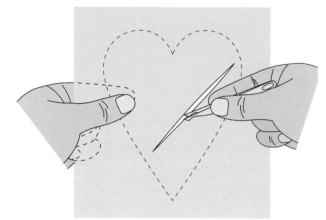

Remove freezer paper after appliqué is complete.

Lesson 1 (page 53) invites you to stay comfortably in your chair by substituting gluestick for the ironing in Prepared Appliqué With Freezer Paper Inside. Two of the "get fancy" options in Lesson 1—adding the acorns and placing a separate reel over the oak leaf sprays—are perfect motifs to do by Prepared Appliqué.

Lessons 5 (page 74) and 6 (page 85) both offer excellent motifs for doing Freezer Paper Inside Appliqué.

Let health and happiness be thy lot,
All I ask is Forget me not.

Straight Talk on Bias

Appliqué patterns are either separate units or papercuts (cut like childhood snowflakes through folded layers of paper). In a papercut patterned block (like those in Lessons 1–5), you transfer the full pattern to a square of appliqué fabric. The pattern shapes fall where they will—on grain or off grain.

With Separate Unit Appliqué, you have choices about where to place the appliqué—choices on which wise women could well disagree. The evidence from old Baltimores is that concern for fabric economy or for clever print use trumps concern for grainline. But how can you, who live amid unprecedented plenty, put the grain to work for you?

When a heart is placed on the grain, the threads stick up at the vulnerable inside corner, just where you want them to lie down. Placed on the bias, however, the same inside corner threads naturally fall where you want them.

When an acorn is placed on the bias, the bias gives a sense of roundness and dimension against the straight grid of the background fabric. Similarly, an ovate leaf is more realistic when placed on the bias, and the curves are easier to turn.

Because it's curved, a wreath stem works best cut on the bias. Start by appliquéing the inside curve of a bias-cut stem. Then sew down the outside, because the bias will stretch to the wider outside diameter. Can a straight-cut stem be made to work for curves? On some antique Baltimore Albums, one can find black check printed on Victoria green wreath stems (used wrong side up, so the black shows little). That long-ago stitcher must have sewn down the wider outside of the wreath first. She must then have sewn the inside, painstakingly close, to ease the fullness—so skillfully that the easement is almost imperceptible and the seam does lie flat. But why didn't she opt for the easier bias stems? Possibly it was for economy. More likely it was a trade-off: The check made it easy to cut the stem's strip, so she chose to use the printed lines as guides. We moderns are blessed with multiple simple ways to cut bias strips—one more thing to be grateful for!

How much does this bias/straight issue matter? Not much. If we were talking cooking here, such fine sensibilities would be more those of lovers of haute cuisine than of those who love hearty American-style home cooking. If you never were to consider bias/straight issues, you, like those Baltimoreans of long ago, would find your own successful way of doing fine appliqué.

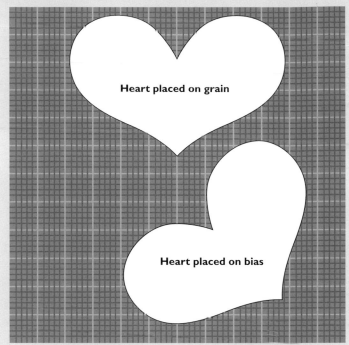

Heart placed on grain

Heart placed on bias

Stray threads are easier to control when heart is cut on bias.

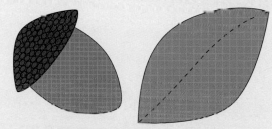

Acorn and leaf placed on bias

Curved stems are easier to stitch when cut on bias.

Nonprepared Appliqué

Needleturn Appliqué

Needleturn is the most familiar form of Nonprepared Appliqué. The seams are not turned under ahead of time; rather, the needle turns under the seam allowance during the appliqué. Needleturn can be used for Separate Unit Appliqués, like the blossoms in Lesson 3 (page 64) or the bird in Lesson 5 (page 78). You can draw the pattern on the appliqué fabric, in which case the drawn line is the turn line. Alternatively, you can cut the appliqué motif from freezer paper and iron it to the right side of the appliqué fabric. In this case, the turn line is actually just beyond the cut edge of the paper.

You can also use Needleturn for connected appliqué shapes. In Baltimores, the most common connected appliqué patterns are papercuts, which are used in Lessons 1 through 5. In Lesson 4, you'll even learn how to make your own papercuts. The ideal way to appliqué papercuts is to use Needleturn Appliqué combined with Cutaway Appliqué.

As lonely through this world I stray,

And pass the pensive hours;

May truth and virtue point the way

And strew my path with flowers.

Where Is the Turn Line?

When a drawn turn line marks a pattern, the needle turns that line under, and that turn line is pretty clear. But when you use a freezer-paper template, the turn line is an imaginary line that is a pencil's width beyond the paper's edge.

- The Cutaway Appliqué cutting process follows the dashed [a] lines on this drawing. Note that a narrower seam allowance is cut over the curves [b].
- On a straight line or on a curve, the stitches are taken in the piping-like fold, 1/16″ beyond the paper's edge [c].
- At an outside point, the last stitch is taken 1 stitch past the paper template [d].
- At an inside point, the cut stops about 3 needle-widths short of the paper [e]. Note that the seam allowance is left wider at an inside point as well.

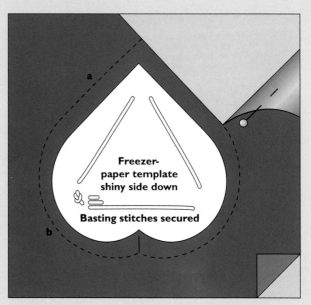

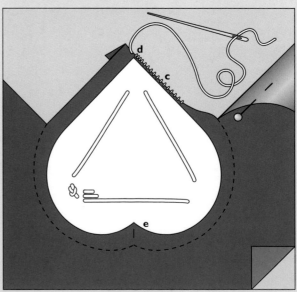

Where's the turn line?

Cutaway Appliqué

In Cutaway Appliqué, the appliqué is cut out—not all at once, but an inch or two at a time—then needleturned under. The advantages are that the uncut fabric keeps the appliqué from shifting and fraying. Cutaway avoids time-consuming basting and allows you to appliqué sooner. The beauty of this method is in its simplicity. Here are its two short rules:

Rule 1 Never cut around a point. Always cut a generous inch past the point whenever possible [a]. Continue that cut in the same direction as the seam.

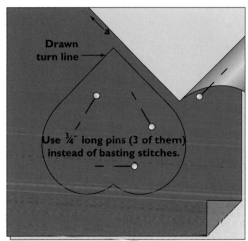

Always cut beyond point.

Rule 2 Never change the direction of your cut until you stitch the first side of a point (or corner) [b].

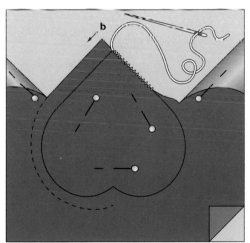

Don't change direction of cut until after point or corner is stitched.

PREPARING A BLOCK FOR CUTAWAY APPLIQUÉ

1. Cut 1 square 9″ × 9″ of background fabric and carefully fold it into quarters, right side out [a]. Do the same for 1 square 9″ × 9″ of appliqué fabric [b]. The crease lines act as registration marks.

2. Transfer the pattern to the appliqué fabric either by drawing it (Method 2, page 116) or by ironing the pattern cut from freezer paper (Method 3, page 117). (To explore another method, see Lesson 2 for Appliqué From the Back.)

3. Layer the pattern-marked appliqué square (right side up) on top of the background square (also right side up.)

4. Pin the layers together in the 4 corners and in the center. Pin from the back [c] to avoid catching the thread as you sew.

5. Put 3 small appliqué pins (from the front [d]) in the area where you'll begin to appliqué. In Method 3, where the freezer-paper template stays on, pin through it too. These pins should be moved ahead as you sew, for they are always securing the area you're sewing. Check the back periodically to ensure that the layers are lying flat.

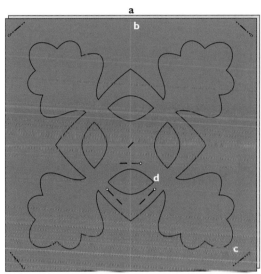

Prepare block for Cutaway Appliqué.

Points, Curves, and Corners

Needleturn rewards practice. It takes skill to turn a fine point, to sweep under a corner, or to stitch a curved seam—but once learned, it gives great joy. For Prepared Appliqué, where the seam-turning has been done beforehand, the stitching is always the same. By contrast, Needleturn Appliqué requires unique techniques for tucking under outside points, creating clean inside corners, and molding rounded curves. Let's learn the secrets of Needleturn Appliqué. As a head start, we'll use the Oak Leaf and Reel Pattern from Lesson 1 to illustrate the basics.

OUTSIDE POINTS

We all like a challenge, and every outside point poses one. Happily, a wonderful formula for turning a perfect point exists. And it works! The illustration shows no freezer-paper template, just a drawn turn line. It also shows a right-hander stitching—all right-handers approach points from the right, whereas left-handers approach from the left.

Appliqué Basics   **23**

Perfect Point Preparation

- Take close, fine (1 needle-width from the fold) stitches for the last ¼˝ before the point [a].
- Take the last stitch right into the drawn turn line itself [b].
- If the lower seam allowance sticks out like a dog-ear [c], clip it off.
- Pull the background fabric firmly over your forefinger beneath the block (The Woven Push [d]). This holds the background still as you move the appliqué seams under the corner.

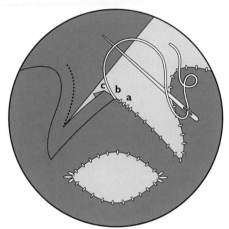

Prepare for perfect point.

Formula for a Perfect Point

Step 1 PUSH

The push takes control of the exposed seam allowances on the point, the ones you want tucked smoothly beneath the point. Always push close to the raw edge and close to the fold, never in the midseam allowance.

A. The Basic Push (my favorite): Push using a round toothpick or the tips of your embroidery scissors. With the sharp tip, push down hard (close to the fold; close to the raw edge) [f] against the seam so the top and bottom seam allowances pivot under as one. This technique gives you greater control for very sharp points and frayed or otherwise difficult points.

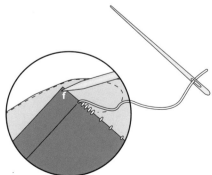

Basic push: use round wooden toothpick or tip of fine embroidery scissors.

B. The Needle Push: Same as A, but use the point of your sewing needle. This technique works for modest points.

C. The Woven Push: Weave the needle in and out of the folded-under seam allowance [e], but not into the background. You'll need a full ³⁄₁₆˝-wide seam allowance to get enough of a bite to work.

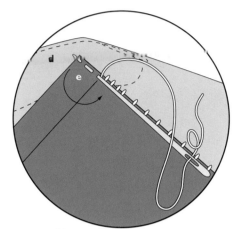

Use needle for woven push.

Step 2 PIVOT

Push down and around, jamming the seam fold to a stop against the sewn seam [g]. Do this with such assurance that the last stitches are loosened [h]. The motion of the pivot is that of making a hospital corner with a bedsheet.

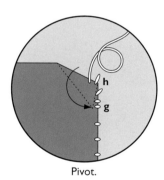

Pivot.

Step 3 PINCH

Completely cover the turned point with your thumb. Because you previously pushed so assertively down and to the right, you can now push, with your thumb pinched to your forefinger, up to the left.

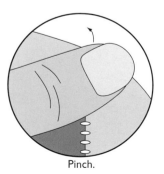

Pinch.

Step 4 PULL

Remove your thumb. If you did everything right, your point will look terribly wrong. The last stitches taken will have been pulled loose [h]. Pull the hanging thread [i]. The fold should magically slip out into a finely turned point.

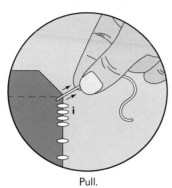

Pull.

Step 5 POINT TO THE POINT

If you've turned the point neatly, you can choose to lock it in place with this stitch: pierce the background 2 threads beyond the point [1], bringing the needle up through the point at [2]. *Note:* Make sure the descent stitches [j] mirror the ascent.

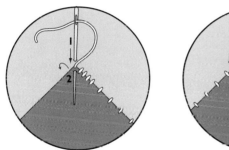
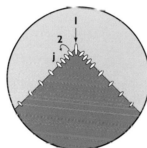

Point to the point.

Elongate the Point

The magical lazy daisy stitch elongates the point.

1. When you get to the stitch at the point, pull the thread to the left and hold it there with your left thumb.

2. Center your needle so it is pointing upward and push it into the appliqué point at [1] to emerge 2 background threads beyond the point at [2], passing over the looped thread [a].

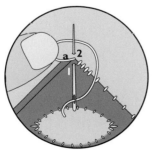

Pass point of needle over
looped thread.

3. Pause and use the point of your closed embroidery scissors (or a toothpick) to tuck under the left seam allowance of the point for about ½" or so [b]. When the slope from the point looks correct, finger-press to crease the seam.

4. Resume by pulling the needle and thread just taut [3], then pierce the background at [4], forming a lazy daisy stitch.

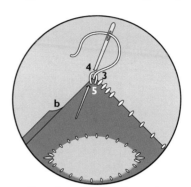

Form lazy daisy stitch at point.

5. Bring the needle up at [5] to begin the first downhill stitch. Make these first downhill stitches mirror the uphill ones in fineness and closeness [c]. *Note:* If done just right, the embroidered lazy daisy stitch gives the impression of a sharper point, especially when done in a 50- or 60-weight thread in the same color as the appliqué.

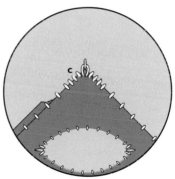

Make descending stitches match ascending stitches.

Pointers for Making Pointier Points

The formula for a perfect point is push, pivot, pinch, pull, and point to the point for…a PERFECT POINT!

Follow these hints for super sharp points, but use caution:

- To reduce the bulk, cut out a wedge from the bottom seam allowance [a] (the seam that has already been sewn).

- To reduce the bulk, cut the seam allowance just $\frac{1}{8}''$ wide [b].

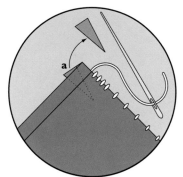

Cut wedge from seam allowance.

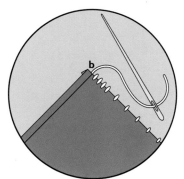

Use $\frac{1}{8}''$ seam allowance.

These super point methods are *dangerous for novices!* Experienced appliquérs become so skilled that they can turn those points on the first try—even if fray starts, it gets turned under. However, this next trick makes almost anything possible!

First Aid for Fray

If you have not had much experience and want to try these risky points, paint the seam cutting line [d] with clear nail polish [c] to seal the threads. Let it dry, then cut the $\frac{1}{8}''$-wide finer seam by cutting through the center of the sealed area [e]. Unlike commercial fabric fray sealers, nail polish does not bleed easily; but be careful not to paint close to the turn line itself.

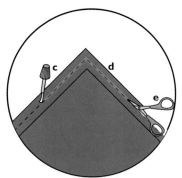

Use nail polish as first aid for fray.

OUTWARD CURVES: SEEKING SLEEK ROLLING HILLS

Unlike patchwork, appliqué positively rollicks with curves. Once an appliquér turns her thoughts to finely sewn curves, she likely will produce them. Why? Because bumps on a curve do not pop up behind what you've just stitched. Bumps on a curve are folds created *before* you sew them in. (If this feels like a guilt trip, fear not: you can avoid it.) Just work out those bumps *before* you sew. Think of the outward curve as a hill that you'll traverse in three stages: climbing up, cresting, and climbing down. Trying to deal with the whole hillock all at once actually leads to peaks in the curve. In Needleturn Appliqué, your thumb holds the part of the curve you've just needleturned under. *The secret on a curve is to stop stitching ⅛″ in front of your thumb so that you can change the direction in which the seam allowance lies beneath the appliqué.*

For alluring curves, try this:

1. Cut a narrower (⅛″) seam allowance on an outside curve [a]. This gives less bulk to turn under.

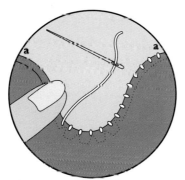

Cut narrower seam allowance on
outside curves.

2. With the point of the needle, catch the seam and pull it under toward you, sweeping your needle from left to right [b] with regal authority—self-confidence helps! Pinch and hold the turned seam to finger-press it.

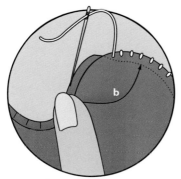

Sweep under seam.

3. Tack stitch to within ⅛″ of your thumb [c]. Stop and lift your thumb so that you can use the point of the needle to catch the turned-under seam allowance [d]. With a windshield wiper–like motion, change the direction of the folds to lie flat. Pinch the curve. Each time you move farther left, work the seam allowance so that the folds follow the changing curve. Follow that curve, one steady stitch at a time.

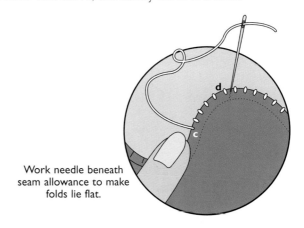

Work needle beneath
seam allowance to make
folds lie flat.

4. If your curve inadvertently peaks, return to the culprit even after the stitching is finished [d, again]. Slip the needle under the seam, use that same windshield-wiper motion to snag the underneath seam on the point of the needle, and pull the seam allowance smooth. Then finger-press it to flat perfection.

INSIDE CURVES: NEEDLETURN PEACEFUL VALLEYS

Use a normal ³⁄₁₆″–⅛″ deep seam allowance on an inside curve. The general rule is to clip the seam allowance. Cut every ¼″ or so, perpendicular to the deepest part of the curve. When the curve is marked with a drawn line, clip to 2 needle-widths short of the drawn line. When a freezer-paper template marks the pattern, clip ⅔ of the seam allowance.

Think of the ¼″ of fabric between clips as a tab [a]. Use the point of the needle to catch the tab and pull it toward you beneath the appliqué. Never place the shank of the needle right in the clip. The object is to turn past the clip so that the

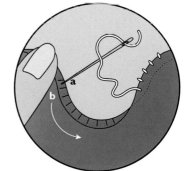

Needleturn inside curves.

clip is swept smoothly under. Start at the top of the curve [b], sweeping under the seam allowance and following close upon that sweep to cover and crease the turn line with your left thumb.

Troubleshooting

- If the valley is a wider one, you may have to needleturn it under once again (by the time you've stitched closer to your thumb), because the turn will have loosened.

- If your clips cause notches, needleturn the *seam-line* under a bit deeper to include the clips in the swept-under seam allowance.

- If your drawn turn line shows after needleturning, your clips need to be deeper. In this case, clip up to, but not *into*, the drawn line.

- If you get tabletops or plateaus (rather than a smooth curve) between clips, you need to cut your clips closer together.

- Try the Gluestick Trick (next page).

Right-Angle Inside Corners:
How Green Was My Valley

Inside corners are fascinating. In my experience, inside corners fit roughly into three main types: Vs, U-turns, and some combination of the two. Each has its customized appliqué approach. The prototype V corner is the right-angle corner—open to the sky, bucolic, and uncomplicated. I think of it fondly as "How green was my valley." Here's how to tackle such a corner.

1. Stop appliquéing ½″ before the corner [a]. Cut into, but not beyond, the corner's turn line [b]. When the corner is symmetrical, as shown, cut to divide the seam allowance in half equally, from one side to the other. *Note:* Remember that when using a freezer-paper template (instead of a drawn line, as shown here), the freezer paper guides the appliqué, and the turn line is ¹⁄₁₆″ beyond the edge of the paper. So here the corner clip [b] would be ¹⁄₁₆″ above the ironed-on freezer-paper template.

2. Rest three-quarters of the needle over the seam allowance flap, with the front quarter [c] moving freely between the appliqué fabric and the background. This way, your needle is positioned to catch and cleanly sweep under that flap.

3. Place your thumb squarely over the corner, so that by pressing thumb to forefinger [d], you can pinch-crease the seam as you sweep it under.

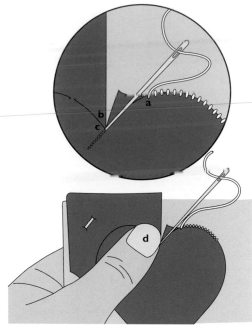

Needleturn inside corner.

4. Lighten your pinch to withdraw the needle, then resume the pressure. Tack-stitch up to your thumb. Nothing different happens [e] until the last stitch before the inside corner [1]. *Note:* The last stitch before an inward corner is begun 3 needle-widths into the appliqué and finishes entering the background under the fold of the seam directly opposite where it began.

5. The stitch at the inward corner begins by coming up 4 needle-widths into the appliqué and finishes going under the seam's fold (but not into the background), coming up through the appliqué fabric again at [2]. It is taken twice, making a loop that—pulled taut—rolls the raw edge under.

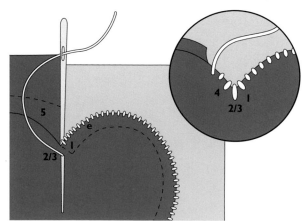

Stitch at inward corner.

6. Cut 1½″ along the dotted line, then needleturn the left side, beginning a ½″ to the left of the inward point [5]. Complete the corner with a 3 needle-width deeper stitch [4].

Like Fingers on a Hand!

The four stitches used on an inside corner are like your three middle fingers. (See Lesson 1, page 50.)

Curing the Impossibly Narrow Inside Corner

- One option is to clip into the corner, short of the turn line. This makes the angle less acute and widens the seam allowance. *Note:* To change the angle, the turn line marking must be impermanent. As an example, use a freezer-paper template to mark the turn line of the original pattern [a]. Then use a silver-colored pencil to trace the outline of the template, lifting the inward point [b] to give enough seam allowance to safely turn the inward point. Notice that the dashed cutting line [c] also shows a narrower seam allowance over the shoulder curve of the heart [d] and a wider seam allowance at the inside corner [e]. Cut into the drawn line [f] and turn under [g] this wider seam allowance. This helps the turned fabric stay under. You are the captain of the appliqué ship—on any pattern, **your** way is the right way.

- Paint the cutting line with clear nail polish [h]. When the V is dry, divide it with a cut [i] into, but not beyond, the turn line [j]. With this technique, the tiny seam allowance turns under more safely and easily, as long as you have not stiffened the turn line with the polish!

- **The Gluestick Trick:** When a fabric frays easily, or with any challenging corner, draw your needle over an open gluestick [k]. When you sweep under the seam allowance [l], the glue comes off onto the seam allowance. Once turned under, the seam allowance will adhere [m] to the background fabric, acting like a third hand and holding it in place while you proceed to stitch under the seam. If you are concerned about a gummed-up needle, pinch the appliqué to the background to clean off the glue as you withdraw the needle.

- Use the lazy daisy way with corner fray. When a thread that is as long as the seam allowance is wide [n] separates from the left seam allowance, consider it a "good fray." Because the thread is long, it will stay tucked after you push it back under. A short fray [o] is more worrisome. After you tuck it under, it might pop out again. Take a lazy daisy stitch to secure the inside point [p]. The lazy daisy leaves 3 threads that act like a dike [q] to hold back any fuzzies.

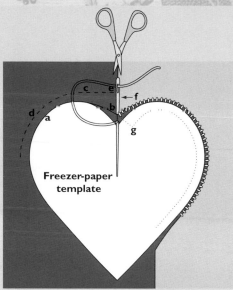

Change angle of corner.

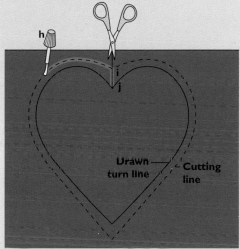

Use nail polish on cutting line.

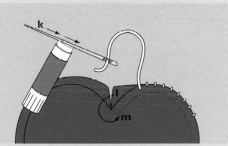

Use the Gluestick Trick.

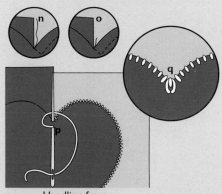

Handling frays

INSIDE CORNERS

Raindrop Corners

Some appliqué corners are all curves, like raindrops or U-turns. Of course, we'll master these, too!

1. When your stitches reach ½″ [a] from the bottom, clip the deepest part of the curve in the shape of a crow's foot [b]. Cut just short of, not *into,* the drawn line [c].

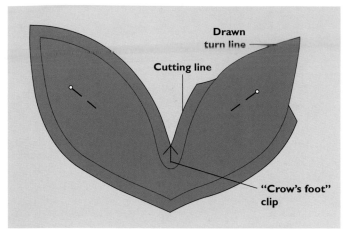

Needleturn U-turn corner.

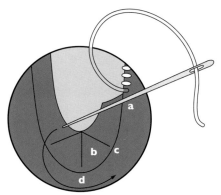

Clip just short of drawn line.

2. Begin above the farthest clip, catching the seam with the tip of the needle and pulling it down and around [d], under the appliqué. Quick as a wink, follow the needle with your thumb, finger-pressing the crease between your thumb and forefinger [e].

3. Continue to finger-press as you stitch toward your thumb, taking a series of normally spaced but deeper (2 needle-widths) stitches [f]. Give a slight tug as you pull each stitch through—you're pulling the fold under, as though you were rolling under the edge of a silk scarf. Midway around the raindrop curve, you may need to repeat Step 2 to keep the seam turned under.

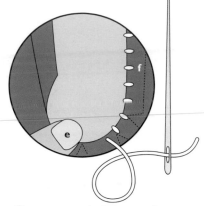

Finger-press and stitch around curve.

Leaf/Stem Corners

A leaf and stem can be cut from one piece of fabric. This simplified construction so appealed to me that I made it the basic technique for stitching the majority of the lessons in *Baltimore Beauties and Beyond: Volume I* (see Courses and Sources, page 173). Now almost two decades later, this technique is more common in our contemporary Albums than in the old Baltimores!

1. Stop when your stitches are ½″ away [a] and cut into the corner turn line at a 45° angle [b].

2. Place the needle in the corner flap. Pinch it between your thumb and forefinger and sweep it down and around [c].

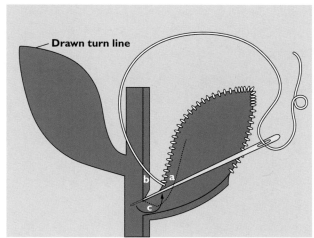

Curved corner meets straight stem.

3. Take a series of slightly deeper (2 needle-widths) stitches until the last stitch before the corner.

4. At the corner, take the deeper (2 needle-widths) stitch directly opposite the slash. Take this stitch twice so that it loops over the edge. Pull it taut so it rolls the corner under [d].

5. Finish the stem side of the corner with one more slightly longer stitch [e].

Finished leaf/stem corner

Basic Embroidery Stitches

This is a small posy of the basic stitches pictured on blocks in this book.

Stem Stitch

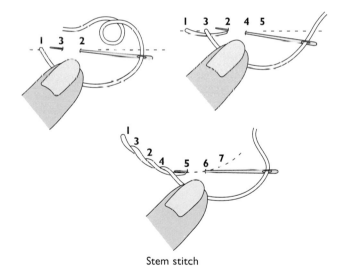

Stem stitch

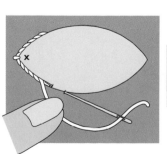

Turning stem stitch corner

Stem stitch (see page 43 for quilt)

Outline Stitch

This mnemonic might help you remember the difference between these first two sister stitches:

Stem Stitch = thread **S**wung low
Outline stitch = thread **O**verhead

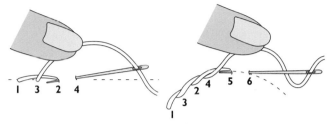

Outline stitch

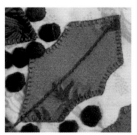

Outline stitch leaf vein
(see page 45 for block)

Couching

This is an amazingly useful embroidery technique. With a single strand of floss, you can draw a fine line. With a double strand or a strand of #8 perle cotton, you can draw a thicker line.

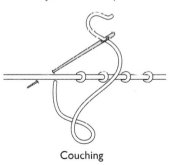

Couching

Couching on bird's nest
(see page 41 for quilt)

Chain Stitch

This stitch is easier to control than the stem or outline stitch.

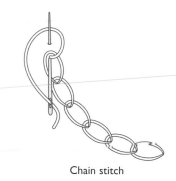

Chain stitch

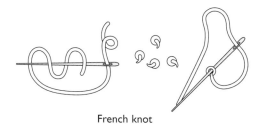

Chain stitch (see page 38 for quilt)

French Knot

This is a simple knot, especially when compared with the Colonial knot (see below). It can be one wrap or multiple wraps.

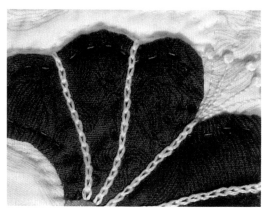

French knot

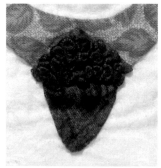

French knot acorn cap
(see page 37 for quilt)

Colonial Knot

This tends to be a more uniform shape than a French knot. Make a figure eight over the needle, as shown. Add another wrap or two for a larger knot.

Colonial knot,
one wrap

Colonial knot, two wraps

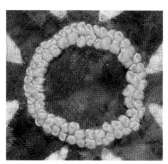

Colonial knots
(see page 44 for quilt)

Satin Stitch

For this filler stitch, first draw on the fabric the outline to be filled (here, the bird's beak from Lesson 5). Take close, but not overlapping, perfectly parallel stitches up in one line and down in the opposite line.

Satin stitch

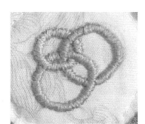

Satin stitched rings
(see page 41 for quilt)

Blanket Stitch

This stitch is a revived 1930s appliqué classic, newly popular because of the ease of fused appliqué. Done by hand or machine, the blanket stitch protects the raw edges of the fused appliqué, just as it protects a buttonhole or the raw edge of a blanket.

What is Fusible Appliqué? Ideal for almost any of the *Baltimore Elegance* blocks, this simplest of all appliqué techniques uses paper-backed fusible web. The pattern is traced on the paper side, fused to the wrong side of the appliqué fabric, cut out on the drawn line (no seam allowance added), and fused to the background fabric.

Janice Vaine's machine blanket-stitched fused embellishment decorates her Album Case (page 110) and shows you how dramatic this quick method can be. Follow the manufacturer's simple directions to use Wonder-Under, Heat 'n' Bond Light, or a similar product.

Michele Silberhorn (*Baby, Oh Baby, Baby Baltimore*, page 44) also uses this method, enriching her quilt with all sorts of whimsical dimensional touches.

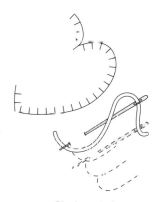

Blanket stitch

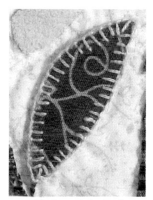

Blanket stitch detail
(see page 42 for quilt)

Feather Stitch

This stitch is sewn from top to bottom. It's perfect for borders, charming in basketry or to vein leaves, and perfect for delightful innovations!

Feather stitch

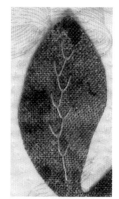

Feather stitch
(see page 41 for quilt)

Raggedy Ann Hairs Stitch

Kathy Gerardi used this unique stitch as part of the sampler of stitches on her Rose of Sharon pattern (see page 43). Make a $\frac{1}{16}$"-long backstitch from outside to inside, leaving a $\frac{1}{2}$"-long loop. Then make a $\frac{1}{16}$" backstitch from inside to outside, leaving a $\frac{1}{2}$" loop. Repeat [a]. Fold the fabric along the backstitch line so you can hold the loops between your thumb and forefinger. Give the loops a $\frac{1}{4}$" haircut and push the hairs to stand upright [b].

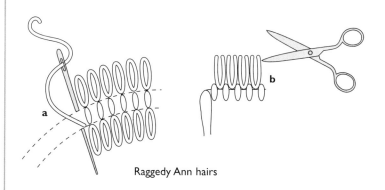

Raggedy Ann hairs

Raggedy Ann hairs in flower center
(see page 43 for quilt)

Of female arts in usefulness
The needle far exceeds the rest,
In ornament there's no device
Affords adornings half so nice.

While thus we practice every art
To adorn and grace our mortal part
Let us with no less care devise
To improve the mind that never dies.

Patterns and Pattern Transfer

How to Take a Pattern From the Book (pages 114–119) begins by teaching you how to take a pattern from this book and then describes different methods for transferring a pattern to a block. Each lesson indicates which pattern transfer method serves that lesson's pattern best. By the last lesson, you will have learned how to approach all the block and border appliqué patterns presented.

Block Completion

Press the Appliqué

Place the block, appliqué side down, on a worn terry-cloth towel. Use an inexpensive (not deeply embossed) paper towel as a pressing cloth. Place it over the wrong side of the block. Lightly spray the paper towel with Magic Sizing spray finish. Magic Sizing inhibits bleeding when you inscribe fabric. Years ago, to my dismay, the cotton appliqué thread bled. To my relief, it bled up into the paper towel, making me a believer in paper towel pressing cloths.

Trim the Block to Size

Place your finished block right side down on a flat surface. Center the 8½″ × 8½″ square gridded ruler or plastic template (see page 12) over the block. Draw the cutting line around the template. Cut out the square.

For machine piecing, the presser foot is a sufficient guide for stitching the ¼″ seam. For hand piecing, you can draw a sewing line ¼″ inside the cut edge using a gridded ruler.

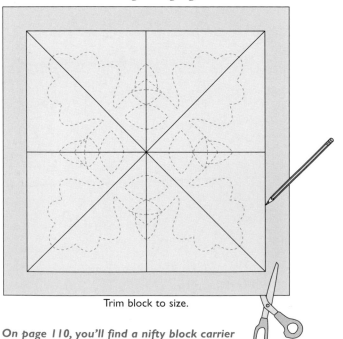

Trim block to size.

On page 110, you'll find a nifty block carrier to store the blocks as you make them.

How to Use This Book

Begin at the beginning. Because each lesson in *Baltimore Elegance* builds upon the one before it, your appliqué cannot help but improve! Are you a beginner? Make the teaching blocks from the early lessons, then tackle one or two of the additional blocks suggested there. Mastering basics eliminates frustration. When you come to patterns that require advanced skills, you have them—or at least you've learned a variety of techniques that unlock the "impossible."

The simplest Album squares are a single appliquéd layer, as in Lesson 1. But you'll soon learn that the skills taught on a simpler shape are the same skills required to do a block as fancy as the paper doily found in Lesson 4. (You'll even learn how to cut original doily-like papercut patterns when you get that far!)

Savor your freedom as you master the fundamentals, then add new skills—as far as the imagination can see. Learn the techniques, find a way, fashion your fancy!

Materials to Begin Each Lesson

Each lesson block requires a 9″ × 9″ background square, appliqué fabric, and the transferred pattern—or the means to transfer it. You'll need basic supplies, including pins (¾″ appliqué pins and 1½″ straight pins or small safety pins to pin appliqué fabric to the background), a fine needle, thread, and scissors. Tools make the difference—the tools and notions list on pages 11–12 provides excellent guidance on scissors, needles, and thread.

Silently, one by one,
In the infinite meadows of heaven
Blossomed the lovely stars,
The forget-me-nots of angels.

Elegant Baltimore Quilts

Sweet Samantha, 36″ × 54″, by Donna Hall Bailey

Family, 42″ × 42″, by Janet R. Costello

My Baby Baltimore,
53″ × 53″,
by Cathy D. Paige, M.D.

Suite Baby Baltimore,
37″ × 37″,
by Lynda Carswell

Baby Baltimore, 42″ × 42″, by Kathy Rankin

Marlena, 33″ × 33″, by Lee Snow, Marjorie Haight Lydecker, Nancy Lydecker Petersons

Jen's Baby Baltimore,
40½″ × 40½″,
by Joyce A. Barone

Basic Baltimore: Angel to Come,
42″ × 34″,
by Karen A. Evans

Quiet Moments, 36½″ × 41½″, by Bette F. Augustine

Baby Blue—Baby Baltimore, 37″ × 37″, by Beverly J. Gamble

United We Stand,
47″ × 47″,
by Nancy P. Wakefield

For Edna and Kathryn,
42½″ × 42½″,
by Kathy Gerardi

Baby, Oh Baby, Baby Baltimore,
44½″ × 54″,
by Michele Silberhorn

To Chris With Love,
51″ × 51″,
by Angie Witting

Reproduction Blocks

The Brickmaker's House, by Mercy Arrastia

Grape and Fig Wreath With Love Birds, by Mercy Arrastia

Vine Wreath of Buds and Blooms, by Yvonne Suutari

Wreath of Holly for Everlasting Life, by Mary K. Tozer

Baltimore's Clipper Ship—The Fastest Ship on the Sea,
by Mary K. Tozer

Truth, Honor & Commitment (Dove and Anchor),
by Darla Jo Hanks

Celebrating Baltimore's Iron Horse, by Donna Hall Bailey

Sweet Soul (Urn of Flowers), by Nadine E. Thompson

Lesson 1

Cathy Paige, M.D. (see page 37 for quilt)

Janet Costello (see page 36 for quilt)

Karen Evans (see page 40 for quilt)

LESSON SUMMARY

Pattern

Oak Leaves and Reel Papercut (Plain or Fancy), Pattern 15 (page 135)

Pattern Transfer

Method 2: Cutaway Appliqué With a Drawn Turn Line (page 116)

Basic Appliqué Techniques

A Cutaway Appliqué With a Drawn Turn Line (pages 22–23)

B Needleturn and Tack Stitch (page 18)

C Inside Curves: Needleturn Peaceful Valleys (page 27)

D Inside Corners (page 30)

E Right-Angle Inside Corners: How Green Was My Valley (page 28)

F Outward Curves: Seeking Sleek Rolling Hills (page 27)

G Formula for a Perfect Point (pages 24–26)

H Leaf/Stem Corners (page 30)

I Prepared Appliqué by Freezer Paper Inside With Gluestick (pages 18–20)

New Techniques in This Lesson

J Separate Unit Appliqué

Basic Embroidery Stitches

K Outline stitch/Stem stitch (page 31)

L French knots/Colonial knots (page 32)

Special Materials Needed for This Lesson

Crewel/embroidery needle size #10

6-strand cotton floss for optional acorn caps

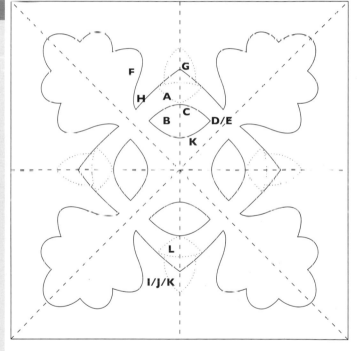

When Cutaway Appliqué entered my life twenty-some years ago, she changed it forever. Though a stitcher since childhood, I became an appliquér when I learned cutaway. And appliqué? To my mind, she is Queen of the Needlearts and the most liberating of stitchery techniques. Our first lesson introduces Needleturn and Cutaway Appliqué, then invites you to follow your fancy. Appliqué's openness to innovation makes her a most fascinating lady!

Block Preparation and Pattern Transfer

Review Materials to Begin Each Lesson (page 34) and Tools and Notions (pages 11–12).

1. Use Method 2: Cutaway Appliqué With a Drawn Turn Line (page 116) to transfer the Oak Leaves and Reel onto a 9″ × 9″ square of green fabric. Trace and cut out the 4 freezer-paper Acorn templates separately and set them aside for Separate Unit Appliqué by Freezer Paper Inside.

2. Prepare the block for Cutaway Appliqué (page 23). Place the marked appliqué square on top of a 9″ × 9″ background square, keeping both squares right side up. Pin the layers together from the back, using 5 anchor pins (safety pins or 1½″ straight pins)—one in each corner of the square and one in the center.

Cutaway Appliqué

The rhythm of Cutaway is cut a little bit, sew a little bit, cut a little bit, and so on. It's peaceful. Though this first block may find you full of questions, by the second block, you'll find appliqué slipping into your soul. Put a bookmark starting at page 23 for reminders of how-to details on points, curves, and inside corners.

We'll warm up by practicing Needleturn Appliqué on the four pumpkin seed shapes at the block's center. Persevere, for when you finish these four isolated shapes, you're in for relaxing, uninterrupted needleturn during your smooth coastal journey along the outline of the Oak Leaves and Reel. You'll be using the tack stitch (page 18), appliqué's most basic stitch. You'll also be able to practice starting and finishing.

Stitching the Pumpkin Seed

Where to Begin the Appliqué?

Stitchers argue, reasonably, that appliqué, like any other physical activity, benefits from a warm-up exercise. In appliqué, this generally means beginning on a long simple area with no tight curves or points or corners. This block offers no easy warm-up, however, so we'll start near the center.

1. To start, pin the appliqué fabric to the background fabric with 3 appliqué pins [a], placed far enough from the edge so the seam allowance can be swept under. Move the pins as you sew (page 23).

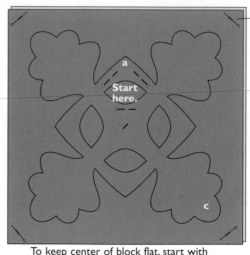

Five anchor pins (pinned from the back) hold layers together.

To keep center of block flat, start with pumpkin seeds.

2. Use fine embroidery scissors to carefully cut a ⅛″ (no more, no less) seam allowance on half of a pumpkin seed [a]. Pin it back to the uncut half [b]. This is the "cut and stitch one side at a time" approach of Cutaway Appliqué.

3. Make 6 evenly spaced clips (approximately every ¼″) into the seam allowance of the curve. Stop each clip 2 needle-widths short of the drawn line [c]. Do not clip into the inside corners yet. You should have 5 tabs. Now you're ready to needleturn!

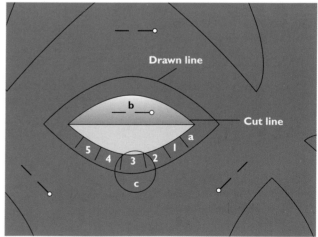

Drawn line

Cut line

To needleturn inside curve, first cut and clip.

Needleturn the Inside Curve

1. Thread a #10 milliner's needle with a fine thread. Knot the end (pages 15–16).

2. To needleturn, use the point of the needle to grab the seam allowance at the top edge, mid-Tab 5, and pull the seam under and *toward* you [a].

3. Use the needle shank to roll under the seam allowance until the drawn line [b] disappears [c]. All in one windshield wiper–like motion, swoop under Tabs 2–5, catching a bit of Tab 1 as you follow the needle with your thumb, finger-pressing the turn into a sharp crease. (See page 28 for troubleshooting inside curves.)

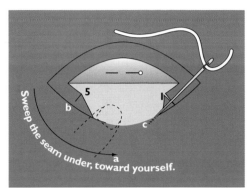

Needleturn inside curve.

Tack Stitch the Inside Curve

1. Tack stitch the turned edge. Taking slightly deeper stitches (2 needle-widths) to help roll under this deep curve, begin stitching to the left of the clip [a] and stitch right to left.

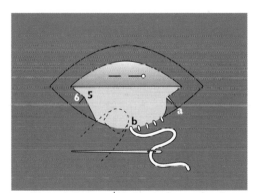

Tack stitch up to ⅛″ ahead of your thumb before stopping to turn under more seam.

2. The general rule is not to sew closer than ⅛″ to your thumb on a curve. So stop stitching [b], lift your thumb, and grab the seam allowance with the needle's point (at the top edge, mid-Tab 6) to needleturn under a bit more seam allow-ance. Continue stitching.

Turn the Corner

1. When you are ½″ from the inside corner, clip into that corner, dividing the seam allowance equally between the left and right seam allowances. Cut into the drawn line, but not beyond it [a]. This clip sets Tab 6 free.

Hint For difficult fabric, use the Gluestick Trick (page 29).

2. Slip the needle into the clipped crack so that its lower portion moves freely beneath the appliqué and its upper three-quarters lie over the corner flap [b].

3. Gently pinch your thumb over the needle [c]. The needle will grab Tab 6 as you sweep the needle to the right [d], pivoting under the seam allowance.

4. Hold the pinch, but withdraw the needle, then resume the same slightly deep tack stitching until you reach your thumb.

5. When you lift your thumb, chances are the corner will look cleanly turned. (If not, sweep the seam allowance under one more time.)

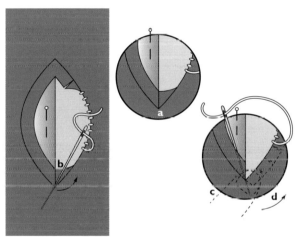

Clip, pinch, then sweep under sharp inside corner.

Tack Stitch the Inside Corner

Continue sewing until you are at the last stitch before the cut on the inside corner. This is Stitch 1 of an inside corner.

LIKE FINGERS ON A HAND!

The four stitches at a sharp inside corner are like your three middle fingers: slightly long, longer still (and taken twice), and slightly long. For a failproof perfect point formula, see Right-Angle Inside Corners: How Green Was My Valley (pages 28–29).

1. *Corner Stitch 1:* Begin this stitch a bit deeper—bring it up through the background through the seam allowance, 3 needle-widths deep inside the appliqué fold [a]. Complete the stitch, reentering straight across from it and under the fold at [b].

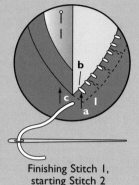

Finishing Stitch 1, starting Stitch 2

2. *Corner Stitch 2:* Begin this even deeper stitch by bringing the needle up (through the background and the appliqué) 4 needle-widths in from the raw-edged corner. Finish Corner Stitch 2 by reentering the background directly opposite at [d]. This time, though, the needle goes under the appliqué only (not the background). Bring it up at [e] (the same place [c] as before). This begins Stitch 3.

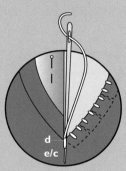

Completing Stitch 2, beginning Stitch 3

3. *Corner Stitch 3:* This is Corner Stitch 2 taken again. Before finishing Stitch 3, park the needle at [a]. Now that you have sewn the first side of the corner, you can cut the seed's remaining seam allowance [b]. Clip Tabs 7–14 [c].

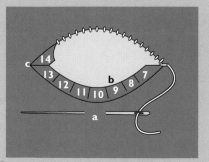

Cut remaining seam allowance and clip curve.

4. Sweep under Tab 7 (starting with the needle's point at mid-Tab 8) before pulling the thread [f] tightly to roll under the raw-edged corner.

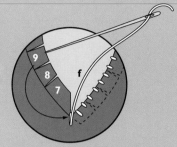

Sweep under mid-Tab 9, Tab 8, and Tab 7.

5. Finish Stitch 3 by going into the background directly under the fold opposite [g] where you brought the needle up. Come up at [h]. This begins Stitch 4 (3 needle-widths deep again).

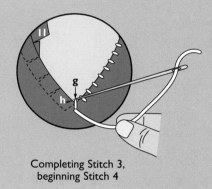

Completing Stitch 3, beginning Stitch 4

6. *Corner Stitch 4:* Complete Stitch 4 (a 2 needle-widths-deep stitch, as in Step 1) and the "third finger" at the corner. Continue 2 needle-width-deep stitches—pulled to roll the edge under—along the fold.

Three fingers at corner

7. Complete the pumpkin seed by turning under the opposite corner when you're ½″ from it and repeating this fingerlike set of stitches.

8. Finish all 4 pumpkin seed shapes, then move on to stitch the outline of the pattern.

Not satisfied with your first seed shape? Know that your appliqué will naturally improve, just like riding a bike. But also know that antique quilts show us a way to clean up unsatisfactory appliqué outlines: simply use 1 strand of 6-strand cotton embroidery thread to embroider a row of Stem Stitch (page 31) snuggled against the appliqué edge. In the old days, this was often done with a single strand of the same sewing thread as was used for the appliqué. When we look at such a fine embroidered line, we sense another's painstaking care, and her affection for the task.

Watch the Leaves Take Shape

Start at an Outside Point

Choose a nonfragile place to start, such as an outside point where you can start sewing ¾″ below it [a]. This makes it easy to tuck under the point from the right side when you come back around to finish the block. You'll be using the first rule of Cutaway Appliqué: Never cut around a point; always cut beyond it (page 23).

1. First move your 3 appliqué pins into place near where you'll start. Remember to move them ahead of you as you sew.
2. Begin with a long cut 1″ beyond the point, running ⅛″ parallel to the turn line and ending ⅛″ from the opposite seam [b].

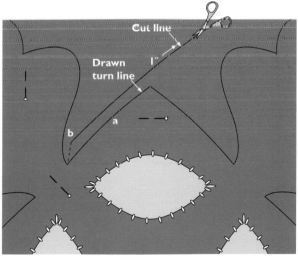

A right-hand start: pin, then cut.

3. Tack stitch to within ½″ of the corner [c], then clip (dividing the seam allowance down the middle) into the corner turn line, but not beyond it. Grab the seam with your needle shank and sweep under the drawn seamline, finger-pressing to crease the turn line. Stop sewing at the last (2 needle-widths deep) stitch before the corner.

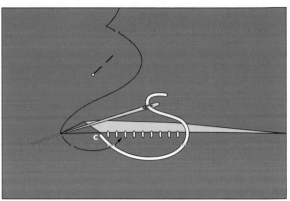

Clip and turn under seam.

4. As in the inside corner of the pumpkin seed (previous page), take your first slightly longer stitch to the right of the corner [a], and then take your second stitch, longer still and taken twice [b], right at the corner. Then park your needle [c] and cut the seam allowance [d] for the first lobe of the adjacent leaf.

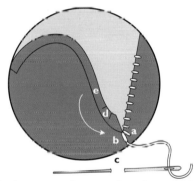

Stitch corner and prepare for adjacent leaf.

The Leaf/Stem Corner

1. A classic Cutaway Leaf/Stem Corner (page 30) is where a straight line meets a curved line. This is such a place. Pull under the curved seam (finger-pressing the needle between your thumb and forefinger), sweeping cleanly from [e] down to the corner.
2. Complete the slightly longer stitch (Corner Stitch 4, 3 needle-widths deep [a on next page]) to the left of the corner. The 4 corner stitches are the same as for the pumpkin seed shape and for a right-angle corner. For this deep curve, though, follow the fourth stitch with a series of 2 needle-width-deep stitches [b on next page] for about ½″. Tug each stitch a bit harder to roll under the curved seam allowance.
3. Outward Curve: As you climb the hill from the Leaf/Stem Corner, you're climbing a Rolling Hills Curve. As the

inside curve becomes an outside curve, the stitches are now the ordinary 1 needle-width deep [c]. Page 27 teaches a simple secret for keeping the curve smooth: Never sew right up to your thumb [d]. Your thumb holds the needle-turned seam as you sew toward it. If you always stop ⅛″ before your stitches reach your thumb, you'll end up with a partially turned area where your needle's windshield-wiper motion can rearrange the ruffled seam allowance beneath the appliqué as you stitch forward. Slow and careful is the motto for tight curves!

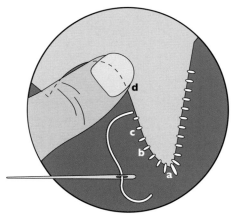

Stitching from inside curve to outside curve

Right-Angle Inside Corner: How Green Was My Valley

1. Stop ½″ before the upcoming inside corner (the valley). This is virtually the same angle as on the pumpkin seeds, so the first one you come to is yet another inside corner (page 28). If it feels familiar, smile and enjoy the moment. This familiarity may well turn to love!

2. Continue stitching up the hills and through the valleys until the leaf meets the reel.

Reels: Making a Point

Reels

A reel is a simple device for winding, more familiar in the olden days. Even when I was a child, movies played by winding from one reel to another. Gone with childhood is the suspense when the movie screeched to a halt and the twisted or broken film had to be fixed before we could watch the end of the story. There was the newsreel, then the feature movie. There is a country dance called the reel. And reel is also a verb, as when the melodrama's villain reels in the hapless damsel. Fishing reels, the ancient tool, are perhaps this recurring quilt motif. They give us something to muse over and make us nostalgic. Times change, but those two contemplative arts—fishing and quilting—still involve the reel!

The Leaf/Stem Corner

1. After taking the middle stitch at the Leaf/Stem Corner, joining the leaf to the reel, it is time to cut the right-hand seam allowance of the reel, ⅛″ parallel to the turn line and 1″ beyond the point [a].

2. Finish the familiar stitches [b and c] of the Leaf/Stem Corner.

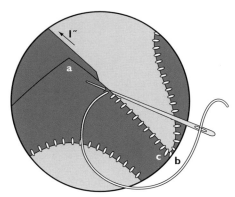

Cut right-hand seam allowance of point, then finish stitching.

The Outside Point

1. Continue needleturning and tack stitching until you are ½″ from this first point. This is a fine time to turn to Formula for a Perfect Point (pages 24–25), where you're instructed to take fine (short) stitches close together for the last ¼″. Because the pattern is drawn on the fabric, take your last stitch right through the drawn line at the point [a].

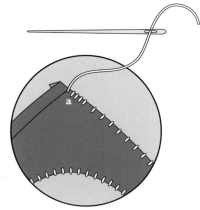

Take last stitch through drawn line at point.

2. Continue, following the perfect point formula on pages 24–25. It is delightfully effective!

What Have You Learned?

By now you will have noted that the stuff of appliqué is points, curves, and inside corners. There are small differences but also wondrously repetitive similarities—wondrous because repetition is how we learn. Success at a new skill is satisfying, but in appliqué, it's rare on the first try. Initially challenging, I wish you pleasing points, because success makes for enjoyable appliqué. The challenge never completely leaves sharp points, though, and the truth is, we appliquérs enjoy the adventure of a good challenge. Our outside points on this block are as easy as any outside corner gets. They are good training for the romantic call of appliqué's death-defying Himalaya-like peaks!

Separate Unit Appliqué

The antique Oak Leaves and Reel Pattern was originally a one-layer, wholecloth papercut design. As a second (top) layer of appliqué, the acorns can be added as an afterthought. What strikes your fancy? Doing them by Ultrasuede Appliqué would be very easy (no seams to turn under!), but those instructions don't come until Lesson 2. Instead, let's walk through appliquéing the acorn nut as a Separate Unit Appliqué prepared by Freezer Paper Inside. But instead of ironing the fabric to the freezer-paper template inside, we'll use gluestick to adhere the seam allowance to the paper template. We'll appliqué the nut and then remove the paper template. We'll finish by embroidering the cap right on the marked background with a cluster of French or Colonial knots, fenced in by the stem stitch. Sounds like our kind of fun!

Freezer Paper Inside (By Gluestick, Not Ironing!)

Review the Prepared Appliqué with Freezer Paper Inside method (pages 18–20). The acorn nut is a great place to try this gluestick version, it's a blessing when no iron is nearby.

ACORN PLACEMENT

1. Mark the placement of each acorn by finger-pressing the appliquéd block into quadrants. The acorns lie over this line with their caps fitted neatly under the pumpkin seed openings.

Folds mark block's vertical and horizontal centers.

2. Cut an acorn template (including the cap) from freezer paper. Mark the vertical center [a].

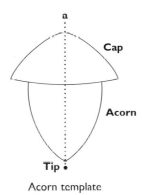

Acorn template

3. Pin the acorn template to the appliquéd block (center line on center line; cap touching the pumpkin seed) and make a dot on the background at the tip of the acorn [b].

4. Cut the cap off the template and trace its outline [c] onto the reel appliqué. Remove and set the template aside.

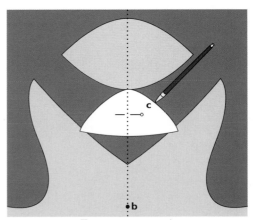

Trace cap onto reel.

PREPARE AND STITCH THE APPLIQUÉ

1. Pin the nut template (freezer paper shiny side up) on the bias to the wrong side of the appliqué fabric.

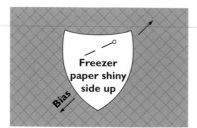

Place template on bias.

2. Cut a ¼″ seam allowance around the nut template.
3. With a gluestick, smear glue on the left and right seam allowance and in an ⅛″-wide area of the adjacent freezer paper [d].
4. Fold the seam allowance point perpendicular to the nut [e].

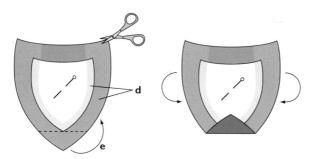

Fold up seam allowance of point.

 The gluey seam adheres firmly to the gluey paper. Fear not—simply give the shiny side of the paper a slight twist to break the seal for easy template removal!

5. Fold the left side, then the right side.

Fold in sides.

6. Use 2 pins to secure the prepared nut to the background. Match the center line and the tip to the dot at [b].

7. Appliqué the acorn from the left side of the nut's raw edge to the raw edge on the right. Use the tack stitch, 1 needle-width deep.

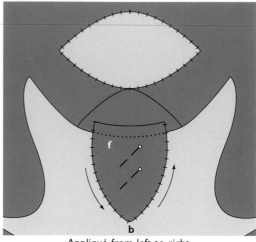

Appliqué from left to right.

8. Draw the bottom line of the cap [f]. Remove the pins.
9. Give the seam allowance a slight twist to break the seal. Hold the seam [g] to keep it from stretching as you tug. Reach in from the top with tweezers to remove the template [h]. The paper will tear free if caught in stitches.

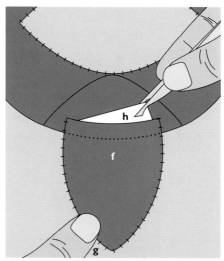

Remove freezer-paper template from acorn.

EMBROIDER THE ACORN CAP

1. Use 2 strands of 6-strand floss in an embroidery needle. Mix a brown and a moss green, for example, to add visual texture.
2. Embroider the drawn outline of the cap, stitching in and out of that line (using the stem stitch from page 31). After the cap is complete, decide whether to stem stitch the nut outline as well. See the fully embroidered acorn on page 32.

3. Embroider the cap with French or Colonial knots (2 strands, 1 wrap). The first row of knots is contiguous to the outline of the cap. Fill in the rest of the cap.

Quickly and easily, you've become familiar with a whole world of appliqué that is quite different from Needleturn! The embroidered embellishment of the acorn and the stem-stitch edging of the pumpkin seed shape are the kind of details that, lifetimes later, bring a smile to the viewer. Congratulations on a deed well done.

Try Different Versions of the Same Pattern

After finishing the Oak Leaves and Reel, consider these additional versions: Make the reel a separate unit out of a different fabric. Make the oak leaves a separate unit laid over, or under, the reel.

Other Patterns to Make Using This Lesson

Wreathed Heart (Pattern 11), Tulip Wreath (Pattern 13), and Tree of Life (Pattern 23); for perfect circles (see page 89).

Other Resources

Appliqué 12 Easy Ways! (Elly Sienkiewicz) offers more appliqué and embroidery stitches and a variety of other ways to appliqué. See Courses and Sources (page 173).

Lynda Carswell (see page 37 for quilt)

Bette F. Augustine (see page 41 for quilt)

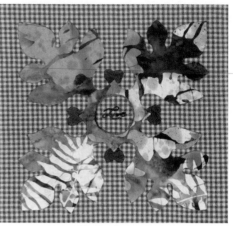

Elly Sienkiewicz

LESSON SUMMARY

Pattern

Hearts and Leaves Papercut, Pattern 14 (page 134)

Pattern Transfer

Method 6: Marking the Wrong Side of the Background (page 118)

Basic Appliqué Techniques

Needleturn and Tack Stitch (page 18)

Cutaway Appliqué (pages 22–23)

Inside Curves: Needleturn Peaceful Valleys (page 27)

Outward Curves: Seeking Sleek Rolling Hills (page 27)

Right-Angle Inside Corners: How Green Was My Valley (page 28)

Prepared Appliqué by Freezer Paper Inside With Gluestick (pages 18–20)

New Techniques in This Lesson

Layered Appliqué (overlap and underlap)

Appliqué From the Back (back-basting)

Miniaturization

Varying the Seam Allowance

Ultrasuede Appliqué

Special Materials Needed for This Lesson

Large-eyed needle, such as a #7 or #8 crewel, chenille, or darner needle

Quilting thread or strand of floss in a contrasting color

Ultrasuede

As a Lesson 1 graduate, you will recognize that this pattern can also be stitched using Cutaway Appliqué with a drawn turn line. Or you can simply do a wholecloth, one-color silhouette of the block, as Bette Augustine has done (page 41). You can even refine and use the Freezer Paper Inside technique from Lesson 1 to make the miniature hearts the top layer of appliqué. Or you can do the little hearts using Ultrasuede Appliqué. (Both Miniaturization and Ultrasuede are taught in this lesson.)

This pattern, which uses techniques from Lesson 1, will surely hone your skills in stitching sharp points and inside curves. If you are a beginner, you should do this lesson's Hearts and Leaves Papercut Pattern using what you learned in Lesson 1 and make the hearts the top layer (rather than following the instructions in this lesson). Doing so will strengthen your skills before progressing to this lesson's more challenging technique.

But if you've already done a lot of appliqué or are ready for something radically different, Lesson 2 teaches a whole new approach.

Where did this different approach come from? More than a decade ago, I heard that a remarkable needleartist, Faye Anderson, appliquéd "from the back." Then word came that another admirable appliqué artist, Jeanna Kimball, was "back-basting." Today this method of transferring the appliqué pattern to the wrong side of the background is all the buzz, especially for experienced appliquérs wanting to try something new. Throughout the years, I had heard the method described so often that I had to try it myself. It was hard to see the basting-marked turn line on the fabric I used, so Laurita Smith, to whom I complained, shared a step that made the method work better for me: draw a line along the basting (as taught on page 58). She also told me that she particularly likes Appliqué From the Back for aligning layered units where precision counts. When stitched beneath the green, the little hearts on this lesson's block certainly fit that description! Furthermore, the theory is that the basting stitches made with a larger needle and a heavier thread perforate the appliqué fabric and teach it to fold under more easily along the pierced turn line.

Block Preparation and Pattern Transfer

Review Materials to Begin Each Lesson (page 34) and Tools and Notions (pages 11–12).

1. Make a full freezer-paper pattern of the Hearts and Leaves Papercut (pages 114 and 134).

2. Use Method 6: Marking the Wrong Side of the Background (page 118) to transfer the pattern to the *wrong side of the background* fabric.

3. Place the background fabric *marked side down* on the table [a]. Ordinarily (and for a one-layer version), you would put the green appliqué fabric over this and pin the 2 together, as in Lesson 1. But for this lesson's method, the fabric for the heart layer comes next (see my block on the previous page).

4. Fold a 4″ × 4″ square of red fabric (for the heart appliqués) diagonally into precise quarters.

5. Place the opened red square on point, right side up on the *right side* of the background fabric [b]. Center the creases over the creases in the background [c].

6. Pin the red fabric in the 4 corners and the center to secure the square in place [d].

7. Use heavier white thread and a large-eyed needle to big-stitch baste the red square to the background, stitching a big X from point to point.

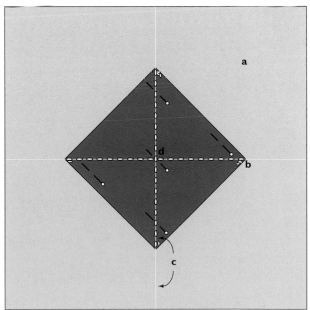

Prepare for heart appliqué.

8. Remove the pins. Now it's time to appliqué from the back.

Layered Appliqué (Overlap and Underlap)

The Hearts and Leaves Papercut is a two-layered appliqué. The bottom (heart) layer must be appliquéd first. Why? Because in our lesson, the leaves are over the hearts. There is no magic to Layered Appliqué. Simply analyze the pattern and judge which layer goes down first. As far as what looks best, the following customary layering sequences come to mind:

- Leaves go over stems
- Buds go under calyxes
- Necks go under collars; heads go over necks
  You get the picture!

Note A seam that gets turned under over another seam is called an *overlap*. A seam that lies flat (unturned) under another layer's turned seam is called an *underlap*. Cut the underlap a full ¼″ wide so it is simpler to cover when the next layer is turned above it.

Appliqué From the Back

Miniatures

Our lesson starts on those tiny hearts—those miniatures. When I was a child, there was an elementary school joke: "How do you dance with a porcupine?" Answer: "Very carefully." So, how do we stitch a miniature heart? Answer: Very carefully! In this case, carefully means finely: a bit smaller on seams and stitches. This is a challenging place to begin a new technique. But from meeting such challenges comes great confidence!

APPLIQUÉ THE HEARTS FIRST

1. Use a large-eyed needle and a white YLI (or other unglazed) quilting thread to baste the heart on the marked wrong side of the background [a]. Begin the basting with a knot in the seam allowance [b] and finish by securing the last stitch [c]. The fine basting stitches should be about ¹⁄₁₆″ long and ¹⁄₁₆″ apart.

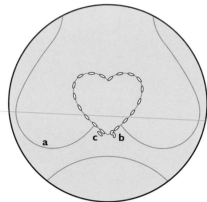

Baste heart from wrong side of background.

2. *Turn over the block to the right side* so you can cut the seam allowances of the hearts. Begin at [d] and trim off the excess red. Note that the width of the seam allowance varies [e]:

- *Sides of the heart:* Cut the seam allowance the normal ⅛″ wide.
- *Outside curves:* Cut a narrower allowance, for less bulk around the curves.
- *Inside corners:* Cut a bit larger allowance to help hold the fabric under at an inside corner.

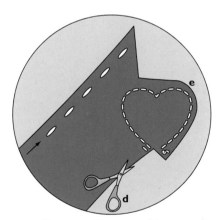

Cut seam allowances of heart.

3. Draw the appliqué turn line just ahead of where you will appliqué next, just outside, but touching, the basting stitches [f]. You'll turn this line under. I use a Pigma .01 or other fine permanent marking pen for this; Laurita uses a soft colored pencil that will eventually rub off. Some who appliqué from the back do not draw the turn line. To experiment, draw the turn line on the first heart you appliqué but not on the second.

4. Snip the basting, clipping every fourth stitch for an inch or so. These hearts are so small, you can go ahead and clip the whole heart at every fourth stitch. With the tip of your needle, pull out enough stitches to free the seam to needle-turn under [g].

5. Start appliquéing at the left bottom of the heart in the underlap [h].

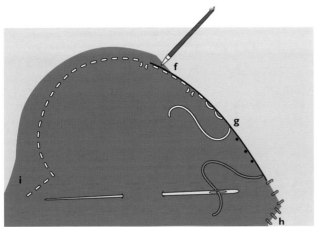

Draw turn line, pull out basting, turn seam under along basting holes, and begin stitching.

6. Refer to Appliqué Basics to perfect the outside curves of each heart (page 27) and the right-angle inside corners (page 28) [i]. One virtue of stitching miniatures is that we are forced to stitch so slowly that we can really savor the process! Complete all 4 hearts, then move on to the leaf layer.

APPLIQUÉ THE LEAF LAYER

1. Place the heart-appliquéd background fabric right side up on the table. Cover it with a 9″ × 9″ square of green fabric, also right side up. Flip the stack over and pin the 4 corners and the center from the back [a]. On the pattern-marked back, put 3 small pins in the area where you'll be basting. Move these pins as you baste.

2. Baste the leaf design from the back side of the background (where you marked the pattern) [b]. Take 1/16″-long stitches on the tight inside curves and outside points. Otherwise your stitches can be about 1/8″ long.

3. Turn the block over, right side up, to begin the appliqué [c].

Inside Circle

Where to begin the appliqué? The inside circle [d] is uncomplicated, so it is a good warm-up place where you can anchor the center of the block. Here you can perfect your inside curves (page 27).

Prepare the appliqué one quadrant of the circle at a time. To review:

1. Draw the turn line (Step 3, previous page), if you like.
2. Clip the seam allowance on the curves every 1/4″, stopping 1/16″ short of the basting holes.
3. Snip every fourth basting stitch.
4. Pull out the first 8 basting stitches or so to get started.
5. Needleturn and appliqué.

Outside Edges

Begin sewing 1″ or so below one of the longest outside points [f] and before a sharp outside corner [g].

1. Cut into the green at [e].
2. Start your appliqué 1″ below the point [f]. If you are right-handed, you'll approach a point from the right. The 1″ that is left open allows you to flip under the point from the right when you come all the way around to finish the block.
3. Snip, remove the stitches (as you did the hearts and circle), and appliqué, inch by inch. The leaf unit has outside points [g and h], raindrop inside corners [i], Peaceful Valley Inside curves [j], and Rolling Hills outward curves [k] (see pages 23–30). The good news is your appliqué will just naturally improve with this beauteous repetition!

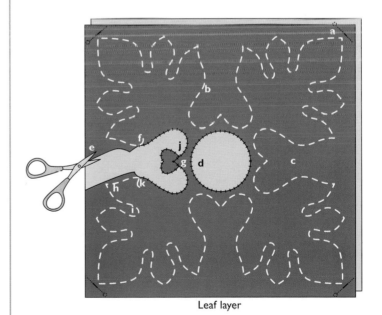

Leaf layer

Ultrasuede Appliqué

If you followed this lesson on back-basting, your hearts would all be finished before you began the leaves. If you chose to do the Hearts and Leaves Papercut Pattern using the Drawn Turn Line on Top method from Lesson 1, you're ready to add the hearts after appliquéing the leaf design [a].

Consider Ultrasuede hearts. Ultrasuede is washable synthetic suede. It needs no added seam allowance, so it is spectacularly easy for sewing miniatures. Because it is polyurethane, however, it must be ironed gingerly (lightly and quickly) with a dry iron set to synthetics. Ultrasuede has a right side (the brighter, nappier side), and you sew it with the same thread and the same tack stitch as for cotton appliqué. In 150 years, someone will be very excited to discover polyurethane in your classic appliqué! Here's how to add Ultrasuede hearts to the leaf appliqué.

1. Iron very lightly (at a low temperature) the freezer-paper heart template, shiny side down, to the right side of the Ultrasuede.
2. Cut around the edge of the heart template [b]. Add no seam allowance. Remove the paper.
3. With a dab of gluestick, glue-baste the heart onto the background.
4. Simply sew it in place with a fine tack stitch [c].

Ultrasuede Appliqué is an easier, alternate way to do miniatures.

As an alternative to Ultrasuede, you can use Robert Kaufman's woven Nu-Suede and sew it with a fine blanket stitch.

Note Ultrasuede takes Pigma pen well for writing or drawing, but the ink must be blotted. It also takes oil pastel stenciled onto it well. In both cases, heat-press it lightly (on the synthetic setting) using a tissue as a pressing cloth to dry and set the color before handling.

Most importantly, Ultrasuede is a tool in your appliqué toolbox. Now that you know how easy Ultrasuede is to use, you can consider it for small, tedious circles or for the fine details of The Mother (Pattern 16, page 136), The Father (Pattern 17, page 137), or anywhere your heart desires. What if you'd rather not do Ultrasuede Appliqué? Well, these hearts could be done by Separate Unit Appliqué With Freezer Paper on Top or Inside. Both techniques are taught in Lesson 3.

What did you think of Appliqué From the Back? By now, you probably realize that each appliqué method works better on one type of pattern than it would on another. Let's continue our exploration of appliqué in Lesson 3. You'll find your own appliqué tastes evolving as you add to your quiver of alternative appliqué arrows!

Try Different Versions of the Same Pattern

Challenge yourself with a different version of the Hearts and Leaves Papercut. Can you figure out how Linda Carswell made the center yellow (see page 56)? There are several possibilities!

Other Patterns to Make Using This Lesson

Red-Tipped Laurel Wreath (Pattern 7), Wreathed Heart (Pattern 11), and Tree of Life (Pattern 23)

Lesson 3

Lynda Carswell (see page 37 for quilt)

Janet Costello (see page 36 for quilt)

Angie Witting (see page 44 for quilt)

LESSON SUMMARY

Pattern

Crossed Flowers, Pattern 2 (page 122)

Pattern Transfer

Method 3: Cutaway Appliqué With Freezer Paper on Top (page 117) for stems and leaves

Method 4: Separate Unit Appliqué With Freezer Paper on Top (page 117) for flowers

Contact paper or self-stick label paper templates (as an alternative to freezer paper)

Basic Appliqué Techniques

Cutaway Appliqué (pages 22–23)

Needleturn and Tack Stitch (page 18)

Separate Unit Appliqué (with Freezer Paper Inside) (page 53)

Outward Curves: Seeking Sleek Rolling Hills (page 27)

Formula for a Perfect Point (pages 24–25)

Raindrop Inside Corner (page 30)

Outside Points (page 23)

New Techniques in This Lesson

Separate Unit Appliqué With Freezer Paper on Top

Perforated Patterns for Transferring Quilting Lines

Pin Placement

Padded Appliqué

Making a One-Layer Motif Into a Multilayer Motif

Sequence in Separate Petal Appliqué

Decorative Topstitching

Special Materials Needed for This Lesson

Thin, dense batting, such as Thermore, for optional padding of the floral appliqué

Embroidery needle and embroidery floss

Self-stick label paper or contact paper, as an alternative to freezer paper (optional)

Our delightful Crossed Flowers Pattern offers a lesson in two Freezer Paper on Top methods. The leaves and stems are done all from one layer of fabric, using Cutaway Appliqué and Needleturn. The flowers are Separate Unit Appliqués done by Needleturn. In both cases, freezer paper on the top marks the finished shape of the appliqué. If you've ever enjoyed the humble pleasures of working a jigsaw puzzle, you'll appreciate how cleverly these on-top freezer-paper templates help you fit the appliqué pieces together! Our lesson focuses on my own favorite way to appliqué: Freezer Paper on Top.

Block Preparation and Pattern Transfer

Review Materials to Begin Each Lesson (page 34) and Tools and Notions (pages 11–12).

For Pattern Transfer Methods 3 and 4, as an alternate to freezer paper, you can photocopy the pattern onto an 8½″ × 11″ uncut sheet of self-stick label paper or trace the pattern onto contact paper using a lightbox. Do the block the same way, but apply the self-stick label paper to the fabric rather than ironing freezer paper to it. Self-stick label paper is available at office supply stores or photocopy shops. Contact paper is sold at variety stores, super stores, and hardware stores.

1. Take the pattern from the book (see pages 114–115 for instructions). Cut out the pattern as a whole, but leave the folded layers stapled together. Cut off the blooms and set them aside. These will be Template B. You'll work first with the leaf/stem unit, Template A.

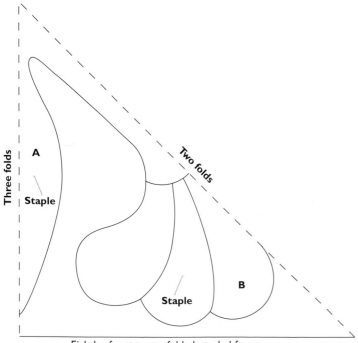

Eighth of pattern on folded, stapled freezer paper

2. Follow the instructions for Pattern Transfer Method 3: Cutaway Appliqué With Freezer Paper on Top (page 117) for the stems and leaves, folding the green appliqué fabric on the diagonal.

3. Prepare the block for Cutaway Appliqué (page 23).

The Leaf Stem Unit by Cutaway Appliqué

A cautionary word about Freezer Paper on Top (see illustration on next page): When using this method, you need to leave a ³⁄₁₆″-deep seam allowance where possible, which is a bit more than the ⅛″ seam allowance the drawn turn line allows. Why? The edge of the freezer-paper template is not the turn line. Rather, it is a guide to the turn line that is ¹⁄₁₆″ beyond the template. When needleturned under, the seamline looks like ¹⁄₁₆″-wide piping [a], or a folded fabric outline showing ¹⁄₁₆″ beyond the cut edge of the freezer paper. So when you clip to an inside corner, clip no closer than a generous ¹⁄₁₆″ from the template edge of the inside corner [b]. You'll roll under that seam allowance's raw edge when you appliqué the corner.

When you turn under an outside corner (a point), you need to stitch the turn line a full ¹⁄₁₆″ beyond the point of the freezer-paper template [c] to keep the piping outline even as you go up and then come back down the mountain that is the point. We'll see these techniques in action as we stitch the leaves and stems. *Note:* Leave the leaf/stem template in place until after you appliqué the blooms and the calyxes.

1. Take the first cut through the appliqué fabric only. This "long handled" cut begins 1″ past the point of the calyx [d]. Note that you start stitching below the dotted line [e]. This leaves the calyx [f] open so you can appliqué the blossom under it after sewing all the greenery.

2. Start sewing with 3 tiny stitches taken right next to each other [e]. These starting stitches lock your appliqué. You won't come back around to them until you finish the calyx by appliquéing it over the completed flower. Begin and end the right and left side of each calyx with these tiny, tight stitches, securing the seams against some stressful handling come blossom time. When you've stitched both sides of a stem, cut the seam allowance of the calyx ³⁄₁₆″ beyond the edge of the freezer paper [g].

3. Continue down the stem, assessing the usefulness of the freezer-paper template. This method takes some getting used to. The freezer paper should be sticking firmly (if it isn't, re-iron with a hot iron, pressing hard at the tip). The paper acts like a third hand, helping you squeeze out that little 1/16" fold so you can take fine, even tack stitches. Keep the piping edge beyond the paper: don't sew so close that the paper obscures your stitching.

4. Sew until you're 1/2" above the raindrop inside corner [h], then stop to clip and turn the corner as described on page 30. Lesson 2 introduced these particular corner personalities, but just to make your day, look what happens to them by eventide: They don a garland of French knots, as though they are dressed for company. Such charm! If the corners have any blemish, it will be the last thing on the minds of the lucky observers. They'll just see a field of bobbing embroidered embellishments.

5. Look at this lovely landscape. On the horizon are rolling hill curves (Outward Curves, page 27), with every so often an inviting mountain peak (Outside Points, page 23). Finish appliquéing all the greenery, then cultivate this vista's blossoms. These might represent cockscombs, a flower beloved of Baltimore Album-makers.

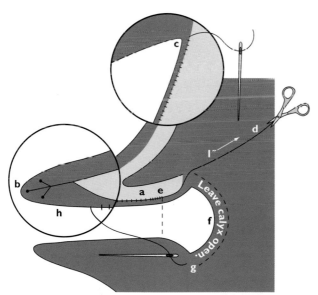

Use Cutaway Appliqué for leaf/stem unit.

Why Freezer Paper on Top?

When you draw a pattern on appliqué fabric, the drawn line is visible until you needleturn it under. When you mark the appliqué pattern with a freezer-paper template, you only imagine that turn-under line 1/16" beyond the freezer paper's edge. In the illustration shown here, this imaginary turn line is shown as a dotted line. One method is not better than another; the method you get used to becomes the best method for you. I learned Cutaway With a Drawn Line but then came to use Freezer Paper on Top more often, because it has these three advantages:

1. Freezer Paper on Top can be a time-saver. When a fraction of the design can be cut through several layers folded together, it quickly produces the full pattern.

2. Freezer Paper on Top acts like a third hand, holding the work steadily against the needleturn's push toward it and keeping the appliqué flat, not puffy or shrunken. I sometimes imagine the freezer paper whispering soothingly, "There, there. There, there." It holds the fabric tightly and aids both seam-turn and stitching.

3. Freezer Paper on Top is highly visible. Highlighted by the bright white freezer paper, the tiny 1/16"-wide fold (the turned seamline) is easy to see. Like the paint-by-number sets of my youth, the freezer-paper guide says, "Needle comes up here between fold and paper [a]. That's exactly right. Good. All's well with the world!"

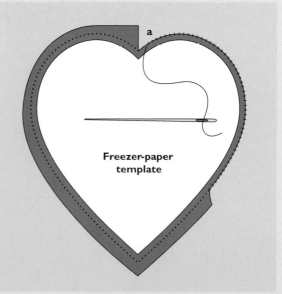

Freezer-paper template

Freezer Paper on Top

Fancy Flowers by Separate Unit Appliqué

Padding the Flowers

Although our lesson models are not padded, these simple flowers invite it. Quilting the flower petals gives the blooms a graceful dimension. If you choose to pad the flowers, do so now, for the floral appliqué follows after. (If you'd rather not pad your blooms, simply disregard these instructions and go to Step 3.) Template C is tailored for cutting the batting; it is a fraction smaller than the finished appliqué shape and has an elongated underlap to gracefully fill the calyx.

1. Make the padding Template C by tracing half of it (actual size below) onto a swatch of freezer paper (folded in half, shiny sides inside). Draw the calyx's top curve [b]. Cut out the template double on the fold [c]. Cut the calyx from its outside curve to ⅛″ from the fold [d] so the template is perforated but still attached.

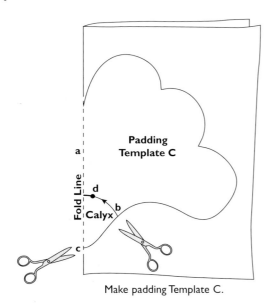

Make padding Template C.

2. Mark the placement of the padding by placing Template C on the background. Pin [e] to align its center fold [f] with the diagonal fold of the background [g]. Use a pin [h] to align the mid-calyx curve of Padding Template C [i] with that of the stem template [j]. Pin the template to the background in 2 places, then trace Template C onto the background [k]. Draw line [d] and the bottom of the Padding Template C by folding back the stem calyx and pinning it out of the way [l]. Mark the padding placement for all 4 blooms.

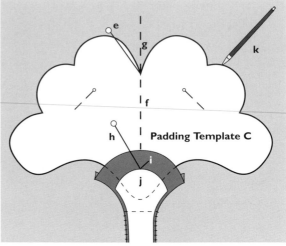

Mark placement of padding on background.

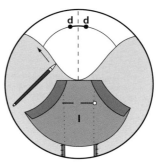

Fold stem calyx and pin out of way.

3. Use Template B (the flower appliqué from the pattern) to minimally mark the flowers on the background, following the careful placement instructions for Template C. Simply put a dot on the background to mark the 6 alignment points on Template B [m]. The padding [n] will easily be covered. Mark all 4 flower positions. If you want more reassurance as to the precise placement, go to Pattern Transfer Method 7: Pattern Veil (pages 118–119) or use a lightbox as described in Additional Methods (page 119).

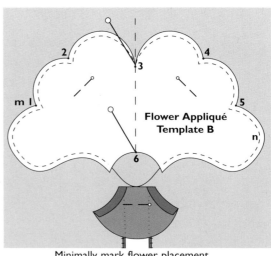

Minimally mark flower placement.

4. Use a Pigma pen to draw Template C 4 times on thin batting. Cut out the padding on the drawn line. Smear a short gluestick strip [o], well within the padding placement line on the background. Press the batting shape of the flower into position for the 4 blooms.

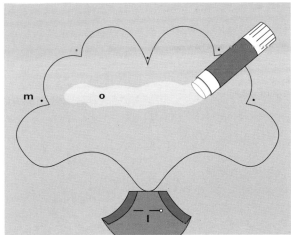

Glue batting in place.

Finish the Floral Appliqué

A perforated template allows you to mark the embroidery and quilting lines without even drawing on the fabric.

1. To prepare all 4 flowers by perforating the flower templates, trace the petal lines onto Template B. Cut each line, first from the top and then from the bottom, leaving 3/16" solid (uncut) in the middle of each line [a].

2. Iron the perforated flower template, shiny side down and on the bias, on the right side of the floral appliqué fabric.

3. Cut a 3/16" seam allowance (or 1/4" for padded appliqué) around all 4 templates [c].

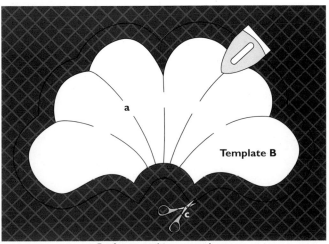

Perforate and iron template.

4. Check the placement by putting a pin through the templated appliqué and aligning it with the dots on the background [d].

5. After the pin-placement check, baste through the paper, the appliqué fabric, the padding, and the background fabric. Big-stitch baste the flower [e] well inside its turn line and remove the pins.

6. Begin Needleturn Appliqué in the underlap [f]. As you stitch around the bloom, practice smooth curves and heed the caution to clip to the turn line, not right up to the paper, on inside curves and corners [g].

Where does the seam allowance go in padded appliqué? It is tucked under the padding [h], like a sheet tucked under a mattress. The generous seam allowance that you have left covers the batting smoothly, without puckering the background fabric. Success!

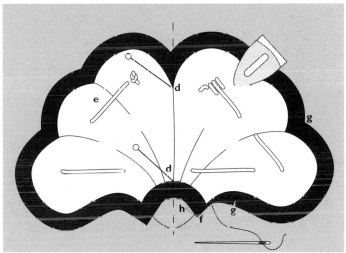

Use pin to check placement, then needleturn.

Appliqué the Calyx and Quilt the Petals

1. After you appliqué the bloom, lift the calyx and pin it into position. Needleturn the overlap, turning under the seam allowance close to the freezer paper. This is the moment when the calyx and flower templates should come elegantly together like a puzzle! If necessary, trim back the freezer paper a tiny bit on the blossom to allow room for stitching [i]. And all those layers? Know that you need catch only the appliqué layer with your appliqué stitches (and soon with your embroidery stitches!).

2. When the appliqué is complete, remove the freezer-paper Template B petals one at a time [j], stitching the quilting line beside each before you remove the next petal [k]. The quilting stitch is really a basting stitch [l]. Because it gets covered with embroidery, it doesn't need to be beautiful. Simply stitch the appliqué fabric through the padding and into the background fabric to quilt the layers.

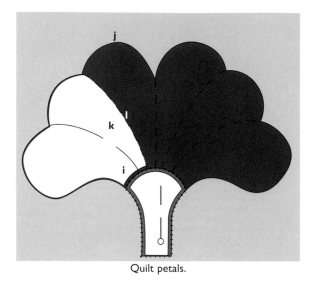

Quilt petals.

Embroidery: The Finishing Touch

1. After you appliqué and quilt the 4 blossoms, embroider over the petal quilting lines with a line of embroidery [m]. Use a close floral color (or a deeper shade of the fabric) and 1 or 2 strands from a 6-strand cotton floss. Choose the stem or chain stitch for the petal lines (see pages 31–32).

2. Optionally or in addition, use the same stitch and color to outline the blossom and a line of green to cap the curved top of the calyx.

3. Embellish the block by chainstitching the stamens in a single strand of embroidery floss [n]. Use Colonial knots at the end [o] (see page 32).

4. Remove the leaf/stem Template A. Save the center circle (Template D) and draw it onto the leaf/stem appliqué.

5. Topstitch the center veins of the leaves. A top stitch is a fine running stitch that looks like the quilting stitch [p] done in cotton sewing thread or a strand of green embroidery floss.

6. Complete the embroidery by outlining the Template D circle, making a row of Colonial knots, with an extra wrap or two, on the inside and outside. Use 2 strands of floss and come up on the drawn line. Why Colonial knots? Once I learned these knots, I found it hard to return to the simpler French knots. But if you prefer French knots, go ahead and use them—they can be just as showy!

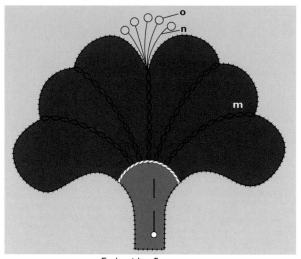

Embroider flowers.

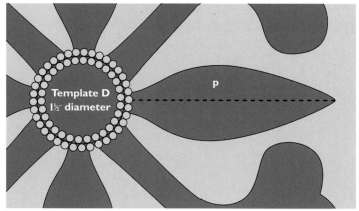

Embroider center and topstitch leaves.

Layered Petals

Lynda Carswell interpreted our one-layer flower as a five petal, two-layer (two-color) appliqué (see pages 37 and 61). Charming! And isn't the effect in the quilt light and colorful? It is a significantly harder approach than this lesson's one-layer flower. Here's how a more advanced appliquér might think through the process:

"I don't think these flowers need to be padded, but I'd like to layer them by piecing them in different colors. Each petal would need an $1/8$" seam allowance all around it. Then I'd pin and piece the petals together in my hand. I'd piece the petals in this order: 2 to 1, then 3 to 2, then 4 to 1, then 5 to 4. Then I'd baste that pieced flower unit in place. When the flower is basted, I'd appliqué it down from right to left [a]."

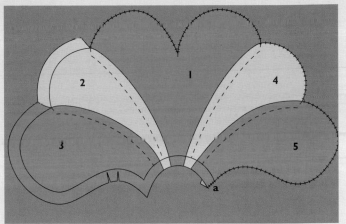

Lynda's layered petals—pieced, then appliquéd

Other Patterns to Make Using This Lesson

Spun Rose (Pattern 1), Crown of Cherries (Pattern 6), Red-Tipped Laurel Wreath (Pattern 7), and Wreathed Heart (Pattern 11)

Karen Evans (see page 40 for quilt)

Michele Silberhorn (see page 44 for quilt)

Cathy Paige, M.D. (see page 37 for quilt)

LESSON SUMMARY

Pattern
Family History Block, Pattern 24 (page 144)

Pattern Transfer
Method 2: Cutaway Appliqué With a Drawn Turn Line
(page 116)

Basic Appliqué Techniques
Cutaway Appliqué With a Drawn Turn Line (pages 22–23)
Needleturn and Tack Stitch (page 18)
Inside Curves: Needleturn Peaceful Valleys for the circle
  (page 27)
Right-Angle Inside Corners: How Green Was My Valley
  (page 28)
Curing the Impossibly Narrow Inside Corner (page 29)

New Techniques in This Lesson
Dogtooth Borders: Antique Template-Free Appliqué
Inscribing in the Copperplate Alphabet
Iron-on Engraving
Silhouettes: Quilt-Perfect Portraiture
Pastel-Stenciled Silhouette
Heat-Transfer Photo Paper
Designing Papercut Patterns

Special Materials Needed for This Lesson
Black Pigma .01 pen
1″-wide masking tape
Photocopy of the engraved banderole (page 71)

Papercut blocks first called me to the Baltimores many long years ago. I was so taken by the simplicity, yet sophistication, of the one-layer blocks! Papercuts are literally patterns cut from one folded sheet of paper. So pulled was I to these quilts that I wrote *Spoken Without a Word,* a book on Baltimore Albums. Later I came to understand that words had, in fact, been penned upon these quilts and that there are all manner of designs and methods in these venerable Albums. Indeed the name *album* implies a collection of differences. To us moderns, this appliqué/inscription mix conveys a certain comforting presence. For me, it conjures up an aura best described by that old-fashioned term *beneficence* (kindliness, goodness, benignity—a blessed presence). Should you, too, wish to pass on some old-fashioned beneficence, inscribable quotations (most from antique needlework) are included on the pattern pages.

Our next lesson introduces an elegant, classic-inspired papercut block. Review the appliqué, then explore the inkwork. Write on your blocks in copperplate calligraphy, use ink silhouette portraiture, iron-on "engraving," or iron-on photocopy transfer paper. The lesson ends with a quick description of designing your own papercuts. Since you now have three lessons under your belt, refer to the lesson summaries as needed for familiar techniques. Let's get started!

Block Preparation and Pattern Transfer

Review Materials to Begin Each Lesson (page 34) and Tools and Notions (pages 11–12).

In appliqué, there is no one right way. This block is a challenge, and you'll gain appliqué practice most easily with a drawn turn line. The instructions and illustrations for how to appliqué this block are based on Pattern Transfer Method 2: Cutaway Appliqué With a Drawn Turn Line.

1. Make a full freezer-paper pattern of the Family History Block (pages 114 and 144).

2. Follow the instructions for Pattern Transfer Method 2: Cutaway Appliqué With a Drawn Turn Line (page 116).

3. Prepare the block for Cutaway Appliqué (page 23).

Cutaway Appliqué

1. Begin the Family History Block at the center. Cut half of the seam allowance of the circle ⅛″ deep [a]. Pin it back to the uncut half [b]. Insert 3 small pins to hold the appliqué in place [c].

2. Clip every ¼″ almost to the drawn line, but not into it [d].

3. Needleturn under the drawn line and tack stitch until you are ready to sew the remaining half-circle.

4. When you're ready for the other half, move the sewing pins into that area. Cut the remaining seam allowance, repeat the clips, and stitch to completion.

5. Stitch the 4 closest triangles [e]. Remember to move your 3 sewing companion pins into this area. These small triangles will slow you, giving you the chance to savor sharp inside points! Consider the gluestick trick as shown on page 29.

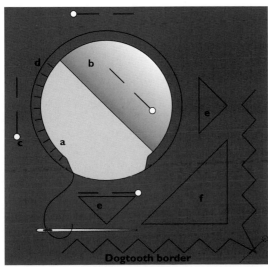

Cutaway appliqué

When you've finished and moved on to the 4 larger triangles [f], you'll feel like an expert. You can rest on your laurels as you enjoy the ease of the dogtooth border.

Dogtooth Borders: Antique Template-Free Appliqué

Our block perimeter has a dogtooth border, or strings of triangles—a common Baltimore Album border. You could practice your Needleturn Appliqué for this border. But before you consider that, read on about dogtooth borders. If you practice them on this block, they will dance in your imagination and become a dramatic, easy solution for bordering your quilt. (See the quilt on page 42.) For now, it shows you a creative way to complete the Family History Block.

When using the template-free method of dogtooth borders, rather than cutting the normal seam allowance up to the points and down to the valleys, you will tuck under the entire triangular seam allowance. Cut a 2½″ × 11″ strip of paper to practice the folding; when doing so, consider how easily you can size and appliqué this sort of border!

Appliqué a Dogtooth Border to a Quilt

1. Pin the strip of fabric for the dogtooth border to the length of the background fabric.

2. Mark off the strip at equal intervals, say 1″. Mark only about 10″ at a time. At every other mark, put a dot ⅛″ from the top edge for the seam allowance [a].

3. At the marks in between, cut down 1½″ on the grainline. Adjust the width of the marks and the depth of the cuts to size the dogteeth as desired.

4. Beginning at the right end, fold under the left side of the first triangle, then fold under the right side of the next triangle. Begin appliquéing in the middle of the first fold and stitch to the base of the triangle. Appliqué up the right side of the adjacent triangle, stopping ⅛″ from the top. Continue in this manner across the strip.

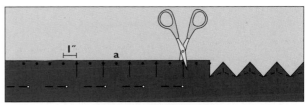

Prepare dogtooth border.

Appliqué a Dogtooth Border to a Block

To apply this technique to this block:

1. Pin the block below the "border" 3 to 5 times.
2. Imagine that each triangle has a number, from 1 at the right corner to 10 at the left. Draw a straight line [a] parallel and ⅛" above the points of the triangles 1–10 and trim it off. Cut into each drawn inside point on the grain, splitting the seam allowance equally between the adjacent triangles [b].

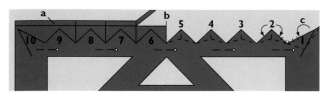

Prepare dogtooth appliqué.

3. Fold under the left side of Triangle 1. Use the shank of your needle to turn under the triangle as you would any angular corner. Then begin the appliqué in the middle of that seam [c].

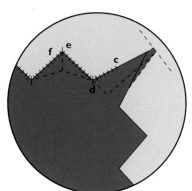

Begin in middle of seam.

4. When you reach the bottom of the valley, take your slightly long stitch, then take the longer stitch of the inside corner twice. Needleturn under the right side of the next triangle to finish the inside point [d], taking close stitches just before the outside point [e], turning the point [f], and so on.
5. The corner point seam is bulkier than the side triangles. Open the seam and clip out the excess as needed.
6. Once you've turned the point of Triangle 1, you've finished the appliqué. Congratulations!

Something to Think About

Contemporary quiltmaker Faye Labanaris made a beautiful dogtooth border to frame a small quilt. The large-scale floral print of the fabric, the large scale of the triangles (about 3″ from point to point and valley to valley), and the 1″-deep base all contributed to the eye-catching, dramatic look of the border. Beverly J. Gamble's blue sashing and dogtooth border (page 42) couldn't be simpler, or more smashing. Hold that thought as a possible border for your *Baltimore Elegance* quilt. The bases of such triangles reveal that they are appliquéd, not pieced.

Ink Embellishment

The open center of this block invites ink embellishing. I prefer to do the inkwork as a finishing touch, after the appliqué is done. It feels right to me—a frosting of the cake. The worst that could happen if you make a mistake is you would have to reverse-appliqué the center to a pre-inked replacement fabric. Of course, you could always ink-embellish the background first, carefully centering the inking on the background block and then centering the appliqué layer precisely over it. Your way is the best way!

Inking Options for the Block Center

You could also transfer a black-and-white line drawing or an engraved image to the center of the block in various ways:

- Spray the wrong side of fabric with Magic Sizing, press to stiffen. Trace drawing or inscription with Pigma .01, press to heat set.
- Use an iron to heat-transfer a photocopy of a black-and-white engraving (see below).
- Freehand inscribe an inscription in elegant copperplate script, using masking tape as a guide line (see page 72).
- Enclose an inked or pastel-stenciled silhouette portrait (see page 72) in an engraved frame or inscription.

HEAT-TRANSFERRED ENGRAVING

You can transfer copies of line art made on many home photocopiers and faxes (not printers). The most basic commercial photocopiers at office supply stores and copy shops also transfer. The technology is changing, though, so avoid inkjet and laser copiers. Try a sample if you aren't sure about the copier. Instructions for using a simple home or office copier follow.

1. Cut a roughly 4″ × 4″ square of freezer paper [a] and iron it, centered and shiny side down, to the wrong side of the background square of the appliqué.

2. Photocopy the banderole and trim it to a ½″ white margin all around.

3. Hold the photocopy to the light and fold it (printed side in) in quarters, creasing it to show the vertical and horizontal center.

4. Pin the photocopy to the background (using 2 pins) [b], copied side down and with creases [c] aligned with the background's quadrant creases [d].

5. Use a dry hot iron (set to linen) and iron on a hard surface. Lift the back end of the iron so that the pressure is hardest on the front end of the iron. Press with a heavy motion to encourage the carbon on the paper to transfer to the fabric. If the iron is scorching hot, protect the background with a tissue abutting the photocopy.

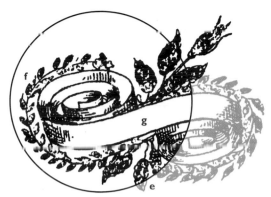

Clarify transferred lines with Pigma pen.

Engraved banderole from printer's die for calling card, found stamped on antique Baltimore Album quilt

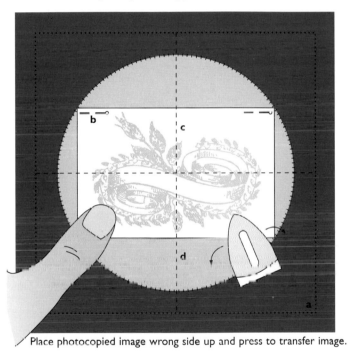

Place photocopied image wrong side up and press to transfer image.

Note Photo-transfer paper, carried by copy shops, office supply stores, and quilt shops, is a good alternative to plain-paper photocopying. Another option is to use pretreated fabric sheets (such as those by Printed Treasures) that you can print on directly with your inkjet printer. (See Courses and Sources on page 173.) Follow the manufacturer's directions.

6. Without removing the pins, lift a corner of the photocopy to see if the print has transferred. If the transfer is not clear, iron hotter and harder. You need enough of an image [e] to be able to draw over it and clarify it.

7. Leave the freezer paper ironed to the back of the background while you go over the photocopy-transferred banderole with a black Pigma .01 pen. Make small, engraving-like pen strokes [f], covering all the imperma-nent photocopy lines with freshly inked lines.

8. After inscribing the banderole's center [g], heat-set the ink, using a tissue as a pressing cloth. Once you complete the pressing, remove the stabilizing freezer paper from the background fabric.

Inscribing Your Block in the Copperplate Hand

The copperplate (or Spencerian) hand is a finishing touch on many nineteenth-century quilts. You can trace this vintage writing over a lightbox onto a block stiffened by Magic Sizing that was sprayed on and ironed from the back. Or you can learn the copperplate script and write it freehand. This script was originally written with a copperplate pen (an elbowed pen still available at art stores). It is now much simpler to use a black Pigma .01 pen to write freehand in the manner of copperplate.

1. If you were taught Palmer script or another slanted writing style as a child, use that script and simply make your writing a bit taller (uppercase three times the lowercase, rather than just two times) and a bit thinner.

2. Thickening each *downstroke* makes a dramatic difference. Practice your name, then practice writing block inscriptions. Ability will follow intent.

3. Use masking tape as a guide line. First do a rough draft directly on the tape, then use the same strip of tape as a straight edge on the fabric and write above it. Lift off the tape, then complete the letter tails that fall below the line.

Copperplate Roundhand Alphabet, by Horace G. Healey
Used with permission of Zaner-Bloser, Inc.

A Footnote to History

One now discredited theory about antique Baltimore Albums was that one or two people did much of the writing on many of the quilts. In the spirit of signing autograph books, I've been honored to sign a great many blocks made or in progress by my students. Signing blocks is a good way to record information for our own historic record. As often as possible, but not always, I inscribe the Latin word scripset, a calligrapher's term, after my signature to show that I wrote it, as opposed to having stitched it. When signing blocks, I'm sometimes asked to write the maker's name. I usually write "By" or "Stitched with love by," but I don't always remember to do this. The mystery of why there are men's names written on many of the old Albums draws different theories. This mystery serves as a good reminder for you and me to put a bit more information, even if only a "By," "For," "In memory of," or "scripset."

Ink a Silhouette Portrait in the Center of Your Block

A silhouette is defined as a filled outline. Silhouettes make quilt-perfect portraiture. Begin with a side-view photograph.

1. Have your subject stand with his or her right shoulder touching the wall, eyes looking up into the far corner of the ceiling, directly ahead. Stand just close enough so that your subject's head almost fills the camera's viewfinder. Take several snapshots. Use a Polaroid or a digital camera for instant results.

2. Print or photocopy the best photograph. Put the copy on a lightbox, picture side down. Work from the blank side and trace the subject's outline. Use a sharp mechanical pencil so you can make corrections. Draw an artistic hairline and neckline. I studied books of silhouettes before I started doing them. It was inspiring to see the small details that added so much to a silhouette portrait.

3. Photocopy the penciled silhouette, then follow the instructions for Heat-Transferred Engraving (see previous pages) to transfer the silhouette to the center of your Family History Block.

4. Fill in the silhouette with ink strokes or fine dots (darker at the outer edge and lighter toward the inside).

5. Alternatively, you can make a sticky paper silhouette template and window template. Use the template to cut a portrait and use Ultrasuede Appliqué (see page 60). Then, use the window template to draw the silhouette outline on the background. Scribble Craypas Specialist Oil Pastels onto the window and use a scrap of muslin pulled over your forefinger to push the pastel colors onto the exposed cloth.

Silhouette window template

Make Your Own Papercut

The Family History Block is an eight-repeat papercut pattern. Eight-repeat patterns outnumber all other forms of papercut appliqué designs and appear to have done so throughout the American quilt's evolution. Making symmetrical mirror-imaged (papercut) block designs is seductively easy. The secret is that the design has to touch from one fold to the other. To try this yourself, follow the directions on page 114. You'll see how easy this Christmas Tree Pattern was to come up with!

1. Fold a 7″ × 7″ square of freezer paper into eighths and then open it up. The eighth you've just marked (C/E) is where your design goes. Make sure the design reaches from the 2-sided fold to the 3-sided fold and connects them even after cutting. Staple inside the design in a couple of areas to keep the layers from shifting.

2. What you draw on the top eighth, even sketchily, can be cut smoothly with good scissors through all 8 layers, then magically unfolded into a more beautiful whole. I keep a pair of the excellent Gingher G5C 5″ craft scissors for making papercut designs.

All schoolchildren well know the delight of cutting snowflakes—whereby cutting a shape through layers transforms plain paper into the mysteries of the universe, captured on a thread or taped to a window. Take an afternoon to enjoy those pleasures once more!

Christmas tree papercut by author

The Stuff of Dreams

When you finish this block (if you've been following the lessons), you'll have completed four blocks. Four blocks make a small quilt. If you set the blocks on point, each within a framing square, and then set these now enlarged blocks together with a sashing (perhaps 3″ wide), then add an inner and an outer border, you'll have a quilt of significant size.

But more than anything, finishing your fourth block signals that it is time to think about what kind of quilt set you'd like to aim for. Look at the finished quilts on pages 35–44. These were all made by volunteer needleartists who chose from the block patterns in this book. Haven't they done a lovely job? It strikes me as brilliant that two of them (see the quilts on pages 36 and 41) chose to duplicate one block four times to create a four-block medallion center. Others (pages 36, 38, 41, and 43) modified block patterns to turn them into border designs. Some (pages 37, 43, and 44) used pieced work elements to create elegant patchwork sets. Since I particularly like papercuts, it occurred to me that some of these papercut designs would make lovely cutaway appliqué borders.

Other Patterns to Make Using This Lesson

Wreathed Heart (Pattern 11), Starburst (Pattern 18), and Star With Tulips (Pattern 19)

Lynda Carswell (see page 37 for quilt)   Cathy Paige, M.D. (see page 37 for quilt)   Bette F. Augustine (see page 41 for quilt)

LESSON SUMMARY

Pattern

Lyre Wreath in Bloom, Pattern 9 (page 129)

Pattern Transfer

Method 3: Cutaway Appliqué With Freezer Paper on Top: Pattern Bridges (page 117)

Method 7: Pattern Veil (pages 118–119)

Method 4: Separate Unit Appliqué With Freezer Paper on Top (page 117)

Basic Appliqué Techniques

Cutaway Appliqué With Freezer Paper on Top (page 63)

Needleturn and Tack Stitch (page 18)

Separate Unit Appliqué (pages 53, 64–65)

Leaf/Stem Corner (page 30)

Right-Angle Inside Corners: How Green Was My Valley (page 28)

Outward Curves: Seeking Sleek Rolling Hills (page 27)

Formula For a Perfect Point (pages 24–25)

New Techniques in This Lesson

Pattern Bridges

Ruching (fabric, ribbon, and Bette Augustine's Gathered Rose)

Bead Embroidery

Split Leaves

Unit Assembly Appliqué (also known as Off-Block Appliqué)

Dimensional Appliqué

Folded Rosebuds (fabric and ribbon)

Ribbon Appliqué (ruched ribbon rose, rake ruching, and fabric ruching)

Special Materials Needed for This Lesson

8″ × 8″ square of PatternEase or other transparent material

2 yards of ⅝″- or ⅞″-wide French shaded wire-edged ribbon (optional for ribbon rose and rosebuds)

Lightweight fusible web

Beginner No More. In following these lessons, you've probably begun to prefer one pattern transfer method or one appliqué technique over another. You should now understand that there are multiple ways to do Cutaway Appliqué. You've learned that Needleturn—that fine art of using your needle to turn under points, curves, and corners—is pretty much the same whether the freezer-paper template remains on top or is drawn around and then removed.

What about the opposite of Cutaway—Separate Unit Appliqué? From the acorns of Lesson 1 with freezer paper inside and the flowers of Lesson 3 with freezer paper on top, you have realized that though their preparation and seam allowance treatment are radically different, both work wonderfully. Our servant in sewing the appliqué to the background—the faithful tack stitch—remains our Steady Eddy. This understanding of consistencies amid differences is a valuable appliqué insight. So celebrate—the time has come for play.

In appliqué, play encourages creativity. Our block for this lesson, the Lyre Wreath in Bloom, introduces us to Dimensional Appliqué, a veritable garden in which to frolic. Free-spirited play invites us into lesser-known techniques, the sort of things that will really thrill the observer 100 or more years from now. It is said that for a work of art to have meaning for the future, it must have the coin of its time. Baltimore Album quilts inspired, but did not give us, the folded circle buds that are Lynda Carswell's one touch of dimension in a classically straightforward block interpretation. Those folded buds came from my own playing, decades ago, and are now a familiar flower of our times. Bette Augustine split her separate unit leaves, a look that comes from a recognizable split print often used in the most sophisticated old Baltimore Albums. Ribbon Appliqué is the coin of the early 1900s and of our time, not of vintage Baltimores. So in the interests of history, we'll consider that fancywork shown in Cathy Paige's block. But first, we'll learn the classic cotton approach to our block.

Block Preparation and Pattern Transfer

Review Materials to Begin Each Lesson (page 34) and Tools and Notions (pages 11–12).

1. Use Method 3: Cutaway Appliqué With Freezer Paper on Top (page 117) to transfer the lyre wreath Template A. Fold a 9″ × 9″ square of freezer paper into fourths. Place the paper opened flat and shiny side down so that the fold lines align over the corresponding fold lines on the pattern.

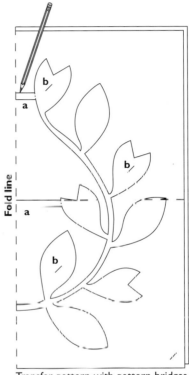

Transfer pattern with pattern bridges.

2. Trace the right half of Template A (the lyre wreath's main stem, with attached leaves, calyxes, and temporary pattern bridges [a]) onto the freezer paper.

3. Refold the paper in half vertically. Staple in 3 places [b] and then cut the tracing lines off Template A as you cut out the pattern, double, on the fold. Otherwise the appliqué would grow, like a sugar cookie in the oven. Leave the pattern bridges attached for now (they will keep the lyre stems in position when the time comes to iron the pattern to the fabric).

4. Prepare the block for Cutaway Appliqué (page 23). *Note:* If you want to inscribe the center of the background, as shown on the pattern, consider doing it before you layer the 2 squares.

5. Clip off the pattern bridges along the dotted line.

Clip off pattern bridges.

6. Position your pins where you'll begin stitching [c]: right-handers begin with a long-handled cut from beyond the point of the top calyx [d] on the left side of the lyre, stopping ½″ before the inside corner at [e].

Block prepared for Cutaway Appliqué

Stop cut ½″ before inside corner.

Cutaway Appliqué

1. Begin with 2 or 3 tiny, tight stitches to lock the point [f]. (This is an exception to the general rule of starting ½″ or so below an outside point. In this instance, you will be sliding in a dimensional bud, as though into a pocket whose 2 top corners are well secured by stitches. You'll see how well it works when you come all the way around the wreath to the opposite point of the calyx at [g].)

2. Tack stitch until you cannot stitch [h] without cutting diagonally into the inside corner.

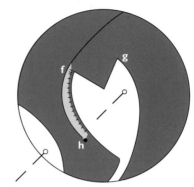

Tack stitch until you need to cut more.

3. Cut into the corner [i] and follow the "fingers on a hand" approach (page 50) to the right-angle inside corner. As you complete the turned corner, look at the straight highway ahead [j]. It leads to a leaf/stem corner [k] (page 30), then to an outward curve rolling hill [l] and an outside point mountain peak [m] that you will turn using the Formula for a Perfect Point (pages 24–25). Then it leads on to a right-angle inside corner [n] (page 28). This geography repeats until you come full around the lyre to crown the first calyx with its bud. Your choice of buds, done in fabric or ribbon, follows.

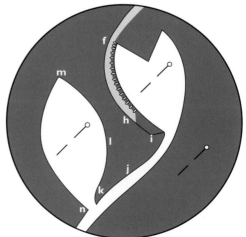

Geography of Cutaway Appliqué

4. When you stitch the opposite point on the calyx, leave the ³/₁₆″-wide seam allowance open, awaiting a bud.

5. If possible, keep the freezer-paper templates in place until you have finished all the appliqué. The freezer-paper templates make it much easier to use the veil transparency placement (coming up on page 78).

Folded Fabric Rosebuds

1. Draw Template B (page 129) on the right side of your fabric. Cut it out, adding ¹/₈″ beyond the circle [a]. Fold the fabric in half. Mark the center of the fold with a pin [b].

2. To reduce the bulk, cut off the top layer ³/₈″ below the fold.

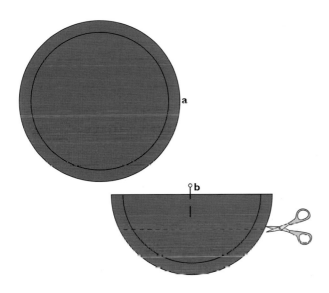

3. Fold from left to right [c], then move over ¹/₈″ and fold from right to left [d]. Pin to hold [e].

4. Use a running stitch along the drawn line and pull to gather—but just a little! Secure the stitches when the bud's width (at a–b) is ⁷/₈″ [f].

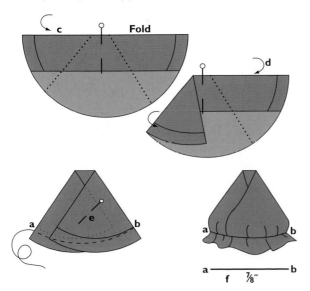

5. Insert small scissors to push the bud into the calyx until the tip of the bud sits about ¹/₄″ above the calyx points [f and g].

6. Tuck under the calyx seam allowance and appliqué the seam to the top layer of the rosebud [h].

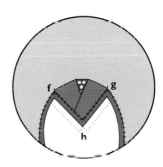

Optional Embellishment

Only the bud tip needs to be tacked down. It can be done either with three Colonial knots (page 32) or seed beads. To stitch a bead flat to the fabric, use a milliner's needle and a strong fine thread (polyester would be ideal) color-matched to the bead. Come up through the center of the bead, then over the outside edge of the bead [i]. Then come up in the center again and then over the other side [j].

No-Sew Folded Wire-Edged Ribbon Rosebuds

You will need 32″ of ⅞″-wide shaded wire-edged ribbon. (This will make eight buds.)

1. For each bud, cut a 4″ piece of the ⅞″-wide ribbon. Insert a pin in the top edge to mark the center [a].

2. Begin a fold ⅛″ to the left of the center pin and fold down to the right [b].

3. Begin the next fold ⅛″ to the right of the center pin [a]. Fold down to the left [c]. This leaves a ¼″ opening at the top [d]. Insert a pin through all layers [e].

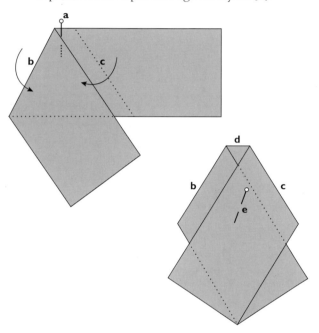

4. Turn over the ribbon so that you're looking at the wired edge marked [f].

5. Put your left thumb over the edge, pinching it between thumb and forefinger as you twist the ribbon tails [g and h] together. (Your pinch keeps the twist from shortening the bud.)

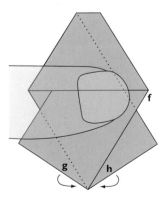

6. Fold up the twist [g/h] so it is behind the bud. This shapes and pads the bud a bit [i].

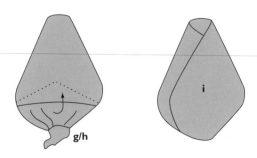

7. Slip the ribbon bud into the calyx and finish it as you would a folded fabric circle bud [j].

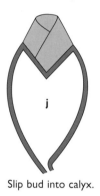

Slip bud into calyx.

The Separate Unit Appliqué

Let's do the separate leaves, bird, and rose by Needleturn Appliqué With Freezer Paper on Top, the method used on the flowers in Lesson 3. This gives us a chance to try the Pattern Veil—a romantic name for a practical placement transparency.

Review Pattern Transfer Method 7: Pattern Veil, also called Transparency Appliqué (pages 118–119). The Lyre Pattern transparency is basted across the top of the partially appliquéd background, the center crease marks are aligned with those on the background, and the bottom is left loose so you can lift it out of the way as needed—just like a veil.

Using the Pattern Veil

1. Make the following freezer-paper templates: 2 of the leaves, Template C; 1 bird, Template D; 1 rose, Template E; and 1 rose center, Template F. Prepare all the separate units in the same way, as described below.

2. Iron the leaf Template C shiny side down and on the bias to the right side of the appliqué fabric.

3. Cut out the leaf with a ³/₁₆″ seam allowance all around.

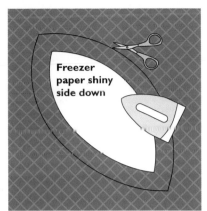

Iron template to right side of fabric
and cut out.

4. Use Pin Placement (pages 117–118) to align the templated leaf underneath its outline [a] on the veil.

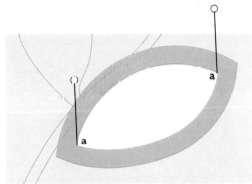

Align leaf underneath marked veil.

5. Pin one side [b] of the templated appliqué through the veil to hold it to the veil. Lower the veil and pin it to the background.

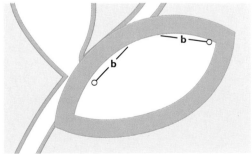

Pin one side of leaf through the veil.

6. Lift the veil enough to pin [c] the leaf appliqué in place on the background.

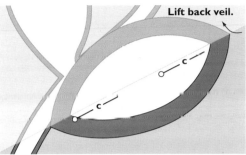

Lift veil and pin leaf in place on background.

7. Unpin the veil and toss it out of the way. Appliqué the leaf in place.

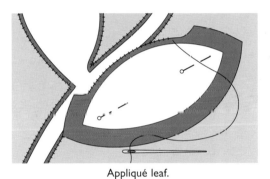

Appliqué leaf.

8. Repeat the previous steps to appliqué the 2-layered bird and the rose. Appliqué the bottom layers to the background first. Note that only the bird's forehead and throat are appliquéd, the unturned seam beneath the beak lies flat. The beak [a] is satin stitched in a single strand of floss (page 32) later. Embroider the legs [b] with 2 strands of 60-weight cotton sewing thread using either the stem or chain stitch. Embroider the feet [c] with the chain stitch or a couched sewing thread. Make the eye [d] from a 2-strand Colonial knot—Bette Augustine used 1 black strand and 1 golden strand, and like a real bird's eye, the eye glows!

Embroidery on bird

Split Leaves by Hand (or Machine)

Split leaves add depth and realism to our greenery. Although this lesson's pattern can accommodate only two of these leaves, Lesson 6 (page 85) has a full wreath of foliage in which such leaves might sprout in glory.

UNIT ASSEMBLY: SPLIT LEAVES BY HAND

Unit Assembly Appliqué involves appliquéing two or more fabric shapes together to make one larger unit to appliqué to the background.

1. Layer 2 coordinated swatches 2″ × 2″ right sides up. Iron the split leaf Template Ca on the top layer and then cutaway appliqué the center vein edge to the bottom layer, beginning ⅛″ within the seam allowance [a].

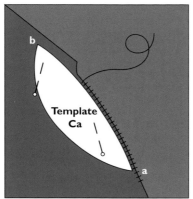

Appliqué center vein edge.

2. When the appliqué is completed ⅛″ into the seam allowance [b], trim the bottom layer so that the seam allowance is a smidgen smaller [c] than the seam allowance on the top Ca layer.

3. Iron Template Cb in place and cut out the completed unit appliqué, adding a ³⁄₁₆″ seam allowance [d].

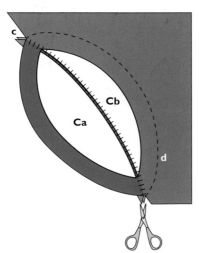

Trim seam allowance.

SPLIT LEAVES BY MACHINE

The fanciest antique Baltimore Albums boast split leaves cut from a stripe—a tan print on one side, a rich blue and green moiré pattern on the other. You can imitate, and even mass-produce, this conceit. Machine sew 2 strips of 2″-wide fabric together with a ⅛″ seam [e]. Try these variations:

- Seam together the right side of one strip to the wrong side of the second strip.

- Seam together one bias-cut strip facing one direction to another facing the opposite direction [f]. Iron open the seam before cutting out the templated appliqué with a ³⁄₁₆″ seam allowance.

Split leaves by machine

Ruching and Roses: A Great Romance!

Ruching and roses are a match made in Baltimore heaven long, long ago. Ruching (pronounced "rooshing") is patterned gathering. Traditional shell ruching is the most familiar. Its name may derive from the fact that each puckered petal (formed by stitching in a mountain/valley pattern) resembles a scallop shell. With variations, this ruching pattern is the basis for both Bette Augustine's rose (see page 83) and my ribbon shell ruching (see pages 81–82).

Shell Ruching in Fabric

1. Iron a 1″ × 22″ strip of lightweight bias fabric in half lengthwise, right sides out.

2. Mark the seam allowance with a dot [a] ¼″ from the right end. To the left of this dot, mark tiny, unobtrusive dots along the fold every 1″. These dots are the peaks of the mountain stitching pattern.

3. On the bottom edge, mark every 1″, beginning ¾″ from the edge. These are the valleys.

4. Thread a milliner's size #10 needle with 20″ of knotted, color-matched, nonslippery thread. Begin below the seam allowance dot and loop the thread over the edge [a], taking ¹⁄₁₆″ running stitches from right to left in a mountain/valley pattern. Throw the thread over whenever you come to the edge. (This loop scallops the edge.) Be careful not to sew through previous stitches—that would prevent gathering.

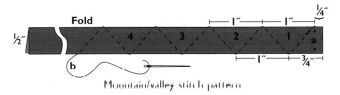

Mountain/valley stitch pattern

5. Stitch 4 complete triangles on the top edge, then pull to gather [b]. Pull tightly enough to form 3½ petals per inch. If desired, shape the petals by pushing them up with embroidery scissors from behind and finger-pressing the perfect petal. Secure the thread before stitching, then gathering 4 more triangles. Note that when you pull to gather, the petals puff up, but the thread of the zigzag stitching pattern becomes an almost straight line of stitches dividing the outer (top) petals from the inner petals! It's a mystery to me.

6. Ruche 25 petals and park the needle [Needle A]. If, after shaping the initial rose, you need to ruche more to finish the flower, do so at this time.

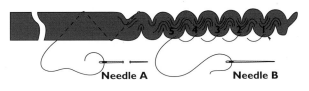

Pull to gather.

7. To form a 5-petal center, stitch together the first 5 petals on the bottom [c]. Pull the thread [Needle B] taut to gather these into a 5-petal center. Secure the thread to lock these in place, but don't cut it. Hold the 5 petals upright, with the ¼″ seam allowance tucked down behind them. Pull up the gathering thread behind the outer row of petals [d] and over to wrap around the juncture between petal 5 and petal 6 three times. Then lock off the thread again, but don't cut it.

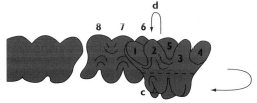

Form a 5-petal center.

8. Open this 5-petal center so it lies flat on the next row of petals. The object is to stitch the outside of a center petal to the gathering line of the petal behind it. After you finish the center, the next row becomes the inner row.

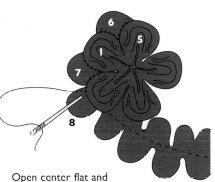

Open center flat and stitch to next row.

Stitch the petals to the center stitch line of the outer row until you have just a few petals left. Tuck the tail of the last petal under the rose and tack it to stay. After embellishing the center, appliqué the outer row of rose petals to the background.

9. One way to finish the rose is to simply embroider a ½″ circle full of Colonial knots (5-strand floss, 1 wrap). Our models have a yellow ½″ circle center. Bette's and Cathy's centers are encircled with colonial knots.

Finished shell ruched rose

Shell Ruching in Ribbon

1. For small-scale ribbon ruching, use a ⅝″-wide French shaded wire-edged ribbon. Cut the ribbon 22″ long. Remove the bottom wire.

2. Leave ¾″ between mountain points on the top and between valleys on the bottom to net 3½ gathered petals per inch.

3. I used a 22″-long ribbon, ruched every ¾″, to make this 2½″-wide rose, which fits our pattern nicely but which could be made larger with a longer ribbon.

4. Use the same technique as for the 5-petal rose center (Step 7, page 81) to make the center, but only use the first three bottom petals. Thread-wrap the juncture between petals 3 and 4. Hold the ruched ribbon strip with the light-colored edge on top, then twist it so the dark-colored edge is on top.

5. To finish, fold forward the 3 center petals, tack them together at the corners, and fill them with colonial knots (5-strand floss, 1 wrap).

Elly's Shell Ruched ribbon rose

Rake Ruching in Ribbon

Cathy Paige's block shows a large five-petal ribbon flower.

1. Use 13½″ of ⅞″-wide ribbon. Remove the bottom wire and seal the cut edges with clear nail polish.

2. For 5 petals, mark with pins every 2½″. Be sure to mark the ¼″ seam allowance at both ends.

3. Stitch the 5 petals. Be careful not to stitch over previous stitches. Pull to gather so the petals fit around a ½″ flower center.

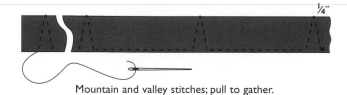

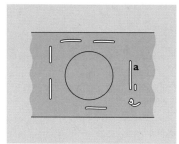

Mountain and valley stitches; pull to gather.

4. Trace Template F (the ½″ flower center) or use a ½″ office dot on a gold-colored ⅞″ × 1¼″ swatch of ribbon. Baste the ribbon in place on the background [a].

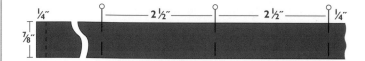

Baste ribbon flower center to background.

5. Baste the 5 gathered flower petals to the background [b]. Carefully appliqué the gathered edge of the petals to the ribbon flower center [c]. Appliqué the outer edge of the 5 flower petals to the background [d]. Wreath the flower center with Colonial knots [e].

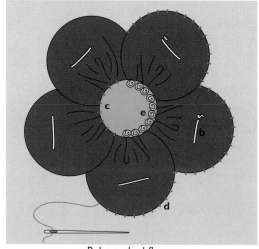

Rake ruched flower

Cathy's quilt (page 37) shows two more patterns made with 4-petal rake ruched blooms. Start with ⅞"-wide, 10½"-long ribbon (or use a 2" x 10½" light-weight cotton bias strip). Make the flowers as described, but gather just four 2½"-wide petals.

Bette Augustine's Gathered Rose

Bette generously shared her original petal instructions, and they work magically. Following these instructions showed me that she took very fine stitches and extraordinary care. She might even have matched valley fold to valley fold when stitching their centers. My circular rose center, made by the traditional method, looks more, well, traditional than hers. Bette's gathered rose is a tour de force and well worth trying if you're looking for an advanced challenge!

Lightly mark the outline of the flower Template E on the background block for placement purposes. To make the first of 5 petals:

1. Cut a bias strip 1" × 4". Fold it in half lengthwise, right sides out.
2. Run a gathering stitch close to the fold. Leave Needle B attached for future gathering.
3. Run a gathering stitch through both layers, from [a] to [b], along the raw edge.

Run gathering stitches close to fold and raw edge.

4. Pull the [a/b] thread to gather the raw edge into a semicircular fan.

Pull to gather into fan.

5. Fold the fan in half so [a] is on top of [b]. With the raw-edge side out, use Needle A to stitch [a] to [b]. Stab-stitch from [a/b] to [d] along the raw-edge gathering line. Knot off at [d].

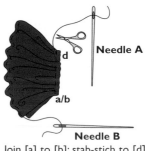

Join [a] to [b]; stab-stich to [d].

6. Carefully pull threaded Needle B to gather the folded edge. Create a rounded petal to fit into your first petal position and pin it in place. When the petal fits, knot off (but do not cut) the thread. The raw edge will lie ¼" inside the dotted line, to be covered by the ruched rose center.

7. With the same threaded Needle B, carefully appliqué the gathered edge, in and out of the valley folds and in and out of the drawn placement line.

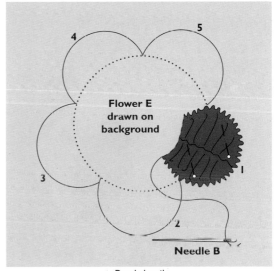

Petal detail

8. Ruche the center of the rose, following the directions (page 81) to shell ruche a 1" × 22" strip. (Trim off the excess after seeing if you need a couple more petals and before tucking the cut end under.) Add this to the first 5 petals for a total of about 19 petals. The diameter will be about 1⅜".

9. Finely sew together the well-formed petals, beginning with the center 5 petals (page 81).

10. Fuse (page 33) a ½″ circle to the ruched rose center. Use Template 1 or a 15mm architect's circle template to cut out the lightweight fusible web-backed fabric. Then draw the embroidery circle on top. Use Template 2 or an 11mm architect's circle template and mark it with a Pigma .01 pen. The fused circle is less bulky than a hemmed circle. It is also sturdier, like a hooped fabric, for embroidery.

Bette's Gathered Rose
fused center

Template patterns for fusible-
backed ruched rose center

11. Wreath the circle center with Colonial knots (5-strand floss, 1 wrap). (See page 32.)

12. Stab-stitch to further sculpt the ruched petal curves, echoing folds only if your muses encourage it!

Other Patterns to Make Using This Lesson

Spun Rose (Pattern 1), Spinning Ruched Roses (Pattern 3), Ruched Hyacinth (Pattern 4), Rake Ruched Rose Wreath (Pattern 5), Crown of Cherries (Pattern 6), Red-Tipped Laurel Wreath (Pattern 7), Crossed Stems With Yo-Yo Roses (Pattern 10), Ruched Rose Heart Wreath (Pattern 12), Wife, Mother, Sister, Daughter, Aunt (Pattern 16), Husband, Father, Brother, Son, Uncle (Pattern 17), Starburst (Pattern 18), Star With Tulips (Pattern 19), Star Rose (Pattern 20), and Squirrel's Berry Breakfast (Pattern 21)

Lynda Carswell (see page 37 for quilt)

Karen Evans (see page 40 for quilt)

Bette F. Augustine (see page 41 for quilt)

LESSON SUMMARY

Patterns

Rose of Sharon, Pattern 8 (page 128); Graduation Basket (pattern in this lesson)

Pattern Transfer

Method 7: Pattern Veil (pages 118–119)

Method 5: Marking the Background Fabric (page 117)

Method 4: Separate Unit Appliqué With Freezer Paper on Top (page 117)

Basic Appliqué Techniques

Cutaway Appliqué With a Drawn Turn Line (pages 22–23)

Needleturn and Tack Stitch (page 18)

Separate Unit Appliqué (page 78)

Pin Placement (pages 117–118)

Outside Points (pages 23–25)

Outward Curves: Seeking Sleek Rolling Hills (page 27)

Inside Curves: Needleturn Peaceful Valleys (pages 27–28)

New Techniques in This Lesson

Folded Square Rosebuds

Embroidered Centers

Perfect Circles

Superfine Stems (made on cloth and in hand)

Basket design and construction

Basic Embroidery Stitches

Colonial Knot (page 32)

Raggedy Ann Hair (page 33)

Special Materials Needed for This Lesson

1 plastic transparency sheet (or 8″ × 8″ piece of PatternEase)

1 uncut sheet of self-stick label paper, freezer paper, or contact paper

Self-stick label dots

Circle template

¼″ masking tape

Cardboard

Basting glue (optional)

This rose is a classic! The Rose of Sharon provides a great last lesson, a familiar must-do-at-least-once grand finale pattern. Beloved, it is a familiar face in the antebellum Baltimore Albums. It predates the Album era—even back then, it was a passed-on tradition. After the Civil War, it became known as the President's Wreath. This simple pattern, inviting so many variations, reminds each stitcher of what has made her who she is.

For centuries, quiltmakers have been passing culture on, just as you and I are doing now: it is part of our art. Wreaths and circles (having no end) bear hints of eternity. The Rose of Sharon is linked with love in the Song of Solomon and would be as appropriate inscribed with a wedding date as with the dates that bracket a beloved's earthly existence. "Let me twine a wreath for thee, Sacred to love and to memory" is my favorite Victorian Album inscription, written, perhaps, *in memoriam*.

As our final lesson, this pattern is taught with Superfine Stems, a new technique for your repertoire. There is then an invitation to linger in the happy world of Album appliqué. Beyond that are specialized techniques for stems and circles, and an original design challenge.

Block Preparation and Pattern Transfer

Review Materials to Begin Each Lesson (page 34) and Tools and Notions (pages 11–12).

1. Review Pattern Transfer Method 7: Pattern Veil. Trace or photocopy the Rose of Sharon Pattern onto an 8½″ × 11″ clear plastic sheet (such as one used to make overhead transparencies). If you prefer, you can trace the pattern onto a square of PatternEase (see pages 118–119).

2. Crease the vertical and horizontal centers into the background cloth square so you can align them with the center of the transparency when you need to place an appliqué.

3. Mark the wreath stem placement by placing the pattern on a lightbox. (See Method 5: Marking the Background Fabric, page 117.) Pin the background square so it is centered over the wreath stem. Trace the outside diameter of the circle on the background fabric.

4. Photocopy the pattern onto an uncut self-stick label sheet. Cut only the 8 leaves, 4 calyxes, and 4 rose templates on

the drawn lines. When the time comes to appliqué, use a long pin to remove the label's protective paper back and stick the template to the right side of the appliqué fabric.

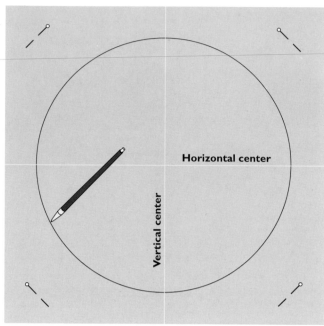

Mark wreath stem placement on background.

Separate Unit Appliqué

Because I love Needleturn, I'm going to teach this lesson using a shortcut version (pattern-photocopied label sheets) of Separate Unit Appliqué With Freezer Paper on Top. If you prefer, you can use Freezer Paper Inside (pages 18–20) for all except the stem on the Rose of Sharon block. This latter method takes some extra preparation time, but it saves appliqué time.

The four folded cotton rosebuds in this lesson are a variation of those in Lesson 5. The stem method in this block is what is left for us to learn in this lesson. By now you understand that there are many methods for preparing and appliquéing a block. The choice is yours.

The calyx lies beneath the wreath stem, and the buds go under the calyx. Thus we'll do the bud/calyx units first. Bette Augustine followed the circle rosebud folding sequence from Lesson 5 (page 77) but made her buds out of 1¾″ × 1¾″ squares. Where I seem to leave a ⅛″ opening at the top of the bud, she leaves a distinctive ⅜″. These preferences become each quiltmaker's elements of style.

Making Bette's Folded Rosebuds

1. Cut 4 squares of fabric 1¾″ × 1¾″. Fold in half [a], right sides out, and mark the center with a pin.
2. Fold the left side in at [b] and the right side in at [c]. (The distance from [b] to [c] is ⅜″). Pin to hold the folds.
3. Do a running stitch from [d] to [e], pulling the thread to gather the bud's width down to ¾″ from [d] to [e]. Secure the thread and cut it.

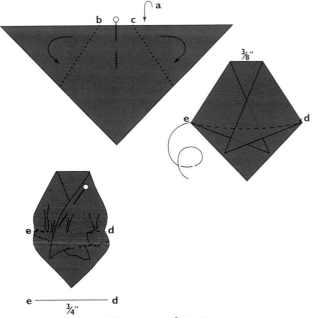

Pin folds; gather to ¾″ width.

Prepare the Calyxes

1. Press the self-stick calyx template to the front of the appliqué fabric on the bias. Cut out the appliqué to include a ³⁄₁₆″ seam allowance beyond the template.

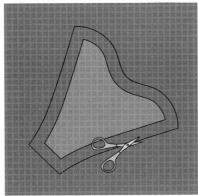

Cut out on bias.

Note Contact paper (with templates traced over a lightbox) is a good substitute for a pattern photocopied onto self-stick label paper. So is freezer paper. To save time, use good scissors and cut out the freezer paper on the drawn line in a stack four layers deep (be sure to staple the layers so they don't shift).

2. Pin the calyx over the bud. Use Pin Placement (pages 117–118) to position the bud/calyx unit beneath the transparency (centered under the diagonal line on the transparency and touching the drawn stem line).

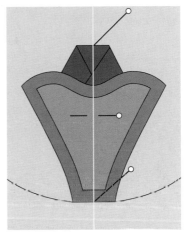

Pin placement of bud/calyx unit

3. Once the bud/calyx unit is in position, pin it to the background in 2 places. Remove the placement pins and set aside the transparency. Begin the calyx appliqué at [a]; finish at [b].

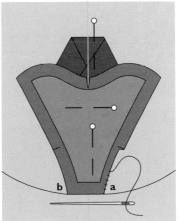

Appliqué calyx.

4. After you sew all 4 bud/calyx units, remove the pins and self-stick templates and then tack the bud tops from behind. The stem, as you can see, comes next.

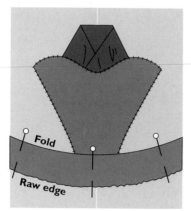

Finished bud with stem pinned
over base of calyx

Superfine Stems

Stems, which I have dubbed Superfine Stems, can be made in-hand or on the background, like this one. The fact that this stem started with such an easy-to-handle strip (1″ wide) charmed me. While the secret to making it superfine is after Step 5, we'll use a classic ¼″ stem.

1. Cut a 1″ × 24″ bias strip of green cotton and fold it in half lengthwise, right sides out.

2. Gently place the bias strip on the background cloth—do not pull it. Orient the fold toward the wreath center with the raw edges right on top of the drawn stem line. Pin the folded stem every 1″, beginning and ending under a yet-to-come rose. (When finished, the folded side will stretch to cover the larger outside of the circle.)

3. Use fine running stitches to stitch a scant ³⁄₁₆″ above and parallel to the raw edges.

4. This is a test: After you've stitched 1″, finger-press the fold, hard up against the stitches and over to cover the raw edges. If the fold covers both the raw edges and the drawn line, finish the running stitches around the circle, then begin tack stitching it down and continue full circle. If not, trim the raw edges back a bit, then finish the circle.

The secret formula: The width of the finished stem is equal to the distance from the running stitches to the fold. To cover the raw edge, make sure the distance to the fold is a bit wider than the distance from the stitches to the raw edges. If the running stitches follow a line ⅛″ parallel to the fold, you can finish (after trimming off the excess) with a ⅛″ wide stem.

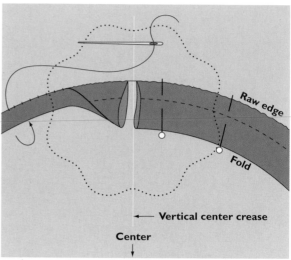

Place and stitch Superfine Stem.

Leaves

1. Prepare the 8 leaves, placing the templates on the bias and cutting them out with a ³⁄₁₆″ seam allowance all around.

2. Use the transparency to position the leaves. Pin them in place.

3. Perfect your formulaic points (pages 24–25)!

Roses

1. Before removing the protective backing from the 4 self-stick rose templates, customize the templates for marking the inner circles:
   - Cut from [A] to [B], then cut from [B] to the right, stopping at dot [b]. This leaves a ¹⁄₁₆″ hinge, which allows you to lift up the circles and draw around the "hole of the donut," as it were, marking the outer center circle. But don't do this until you've appliquéd the perimeter of the rose.
   - Cut from [C] to the right, stopping at dot [c]. This leaves a hinge that allows you to open circle [C] and draw it on the rose appliqué, just before you remove the self-stick templates and embroider the Colonial knot centers. You should recognize this partial cutting as a version of the "perforated template" in Lesson 3 (page 65).

2. Ever so carefully, remove the protective paper from Template A. Don't even bother removing the backing from B and C inner circles. They are fragile; when the time comes to mark the centers, you can finger-press to hold them in place.

3. Press the templates to the rose fabric and cut out each one, including a scant ³⁄₁₆″ seam allowance (scant because of the tight curves.)

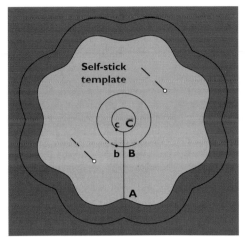

Press templates to fabric.

4. Use the transparency to place and pin a rose in position, then appliqué the outside edge. Take particular care to define the valleys by stitching close to the paper. Give yourself a boost by skimming Outward Curves: Seeking Sleek Rolling Hills (page 27) and Inside Curves: Needleturn Peaceful Valleys (pages 27–28). Enjoy the countryside!

5. To make the inner circles, remove the backing from Template C and trace the perimeter with a black Pigma .01 pen. I like to use an architect's circle template because it is rigid and easier to trace around than the template. However, the template gives you the placement. Template C is the same as a 9mm architect's circle, and Template B is 15mm or ½″. Remove the backing from Template B and draw the perimeter.

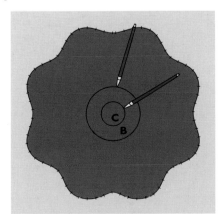

Draw B and C circles.

6. For Bette's version of the flower center (page 85), first embroider Colonial knots on line [C] (2 wraps with 1 dark strand and 1 lighter strand) by coming up on the drawn line, reentering the fabric toward the center, and filling in to line B. Embroider the center of Template C with French knots (1 strand, 2 wraps). For Karen Evans's version (page 85), simply embroider line [B] with a row of Colonial knots (6 strands, 1 wrap), then embroider line [C] similarly.

7. For an alternative to the appliquéd circle center, such as Lynda Carswell did (page 85), appliqué the 2 circles in the rose center. The perforated template concept (page 65) is a boon for placing these appliqués.

A Word on Circles

You can needleturn any circle. The proof is in Mary Tozer's ¹⁄₈″ needleturned holly wreath berries (page 45). It is slow going, but there are a number of other methods, too.

- Use a freezer-paper or self-stick template on top to help control the edge.

- Gather the seam allowance of the circle up, over, and around a file card circle; spray with Magic Sizing; iron from the wrong side; clip the thread; and then pop out the file card circle.

- Use Mylar washers from the hardware store (precut perfect circles that come in many sizes), just like the file card circles (described above).

- Place a self-stick label dot (from an office supply store) sticky side up on the wrong side of the fabric, trim off a ¹⁄₈″ seam allowance, and push the allowance down carefully all around (with embroidery scissors) so it is held by the sticky side. These dots come in sizes from ¹⁄₈″ to 1″ in diameter. The only way to remove them is to slit the back of the appliqué and use tweezers to pull them out. Where there's a will, there's a way!

Top Stitch and Embroidery Options

Topstitching is the running stitch taken through the appliqué and the background cloth. This stitch can draw the center vein on these simple leaves or define them a bit. The pattern suggests that you could also topstitch the rose to define its petals in more detail. I'm particularly fond of topstitching leaves. Kathy Gerardi made her Rose of Sharon Wreath (page 43) a sampler of different centers, combining a laid basketweave (a version of the satin stitch), Colonial knots, and Raggedy Ann hair, all taught in Basic Embroidery Stitches (pages 31–33).

Star-Spangled Stem Review

As with making circles, everyone has a favorite stem. I share my favorites here. Superfine Stems are excellent, but they have to be sewn to the background as you make them. They can't be woven into baskets or arranged freely to fill a vase. To do this, you need premade stems.

Stems Made in-Hand

Marjorie Mahoney taught me this wonderfully easy stem—by phone! You could use this trifold, basted strip to make any stem, including the Rose of Sharon stem. In addition—and this is big—you can also use it to weave a basket or to sew a meandering stem of inside and outside curves (as on a border). Simply sew the inside curves first and allow the bias to stretch to the outside. The finest stems can be knotted in a basket.

Basic numbers: A 1″-wide strip makes a $^5/_{16}$″-wide stem; a $^7/_8$″-wide strip makes a $^1/_4$″-wide stem; and a $^3/_4$″-wide strip makes a $^3/_{16}$″-wide stem.

1. With the wrong side of the fabric facing up, fold a 1″ stem in thirds (left to right [a], right to left [b]). It is now folded right sides out, and you're looking at the wrong side of the stem—the side that goes against the background. Pin once at the top [c].
2. Hold the strip in your left hand. With your right hand, baste the length of the strip. Use a #10 milliner's needle with a strong, nonslippery thread and take $^1/_8$″- to $^3/_{16}$″-long basting stitches.
3. When you need to cut a length off the strip, pin a channel and cut [d]. (The pins keep the basting from coming out until you need to cut off more stem.)

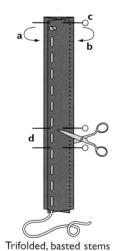

Trifolded, basted stems

4. Place the stem right side up and pin it in place on the background, with one edge just covering the drawn placement line [e]. With this trifold stem, appliqué the inside of a curve first [f]. The other fold will stretch to cover the outside curve. Once both stem sides are appliquéd, pull out the basting stitches [g].

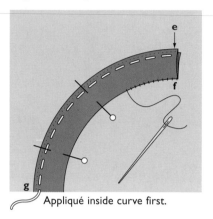

Appliqué inside curve first.

CAN A TRIFOLD STEM FINISH $^1/_8$″ WIDE?

Yes. Iron a 1″-wide strip in half, right sides out. Trim the top layer to $^1/_8$″ from the fold to the cut edge. Trim the bottom layer to $^1/_4$″. The ironed fold gives you control to fold this in thirds in your hands. Baste with a #11 milliner's needle and 60-weight cotton thread—use these fine tools so you don't chew up the stem with the basting.

AND FOR A CIRCLE WITHOUT END?

If you have no way to hide the beginning and end of a wreath stem under something, a clean way to hide it would be to iron the seam up and over a Freezer Paper Inside (pages 18–20) full circular stem. On a wreath the size of our Rose of Sharon, this should be easy!

Baskets

Baskets held blessings in Baltimore's Albums. Our Thanksgiving cornucopia echoes this symbolism. With those folded stems now part of our repertoire, we can take a quick look at the anatomy of a basket and almost intuitively be able to make a Graduation Basket (page 92) to hold all the flora we've learned.

The Anatomy of a Basket

The baskets pictured here all have *frames* around a *center window* opening, behind which lies a *foundation fabric* and/or the ribs and weavers.

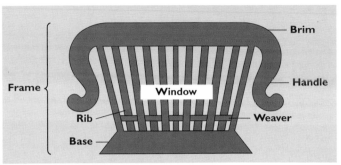

Anatomy of a basket

WHERE TO WEAVE YOUR BASKETS

You can weave your basket directly on the background fabric above. Or you can weave it on the foundation: a different fabric cut ¼″ larger all around (the underlap) than the window [a] and basted to the background. Put dots in the four corners as registration marks for pin-placing the frame [b]. The foundation fabric will lie under the frame and over the background fabric.

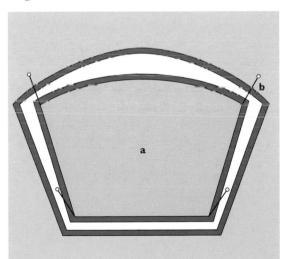

Foundation fabric under frame and over background

THE RIBS

The ribs run vertically and are pinned onto the foundation first. Work with a cardboard work surface beneath the background, with the foundation shape basted over it. Pin the ribs (and later the weavers) to the cardboard as you would a butterfly collection. Use basting glue or ¼″ masking tape to hold the ribs in place for appliqué. You could even have a design of only ribs.

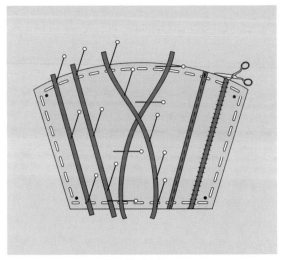

Pin ribs in place.

THE WEAVERS

The weavers move (horizontally) in and out of a basket's ribs. An odd number of ribs means the weavers finish the same on the basket's left and right [c]. Lay out the weavers as you would the strips of a lattice pie crust: First pull back the even-numbered ribs and place a weaver over the remaining odd-numbered ones. Now pull the folded weavers back up. Voilà! Continue odd number, even number for however many rows you want to weave. Pin and baste them in place, then appliqué one, or both sides of the ribs and weavers to the foundation cloth.

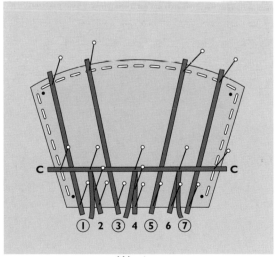

Weaving

THE FRAME

Prepare the frame with Freezer Paper on Top. Use Pin Placement to center the window frame over the foundation. Pin and baste, and then appliqué the frame in place and remove the paper. Impressive!

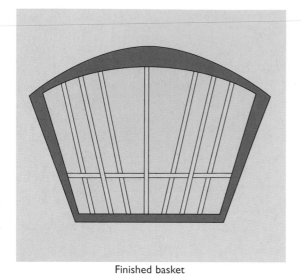

Finished basket

TO FILL THE BASKET

Design a bouquet for your basket over a 7″ square of paper clearly marked with a 6½″ diameter circle centered on it. Arrange the leaf/bloom cutouts on paper or on a background over a lightbox using the circular outline to shape the bouquet.

Other Patterns to Make Using This Lesson

Spun Rose (Pattern 1), Spinning Ruched Roses (Pattern 3), Ruched Hyacinth (Pattern 4), Crown of Cherries (Pattern 6), Crossed Stems With Yo-Yo Roses (Pattern 10), Wife, Mother, Sister, Daughter, Aunt (Pattern 16), Husband, Father, Brother, Son, Uncle (Pattern 17), Star Rose (Pattern 20), and Squirrel's Berry Breakfast (Pattern 21)

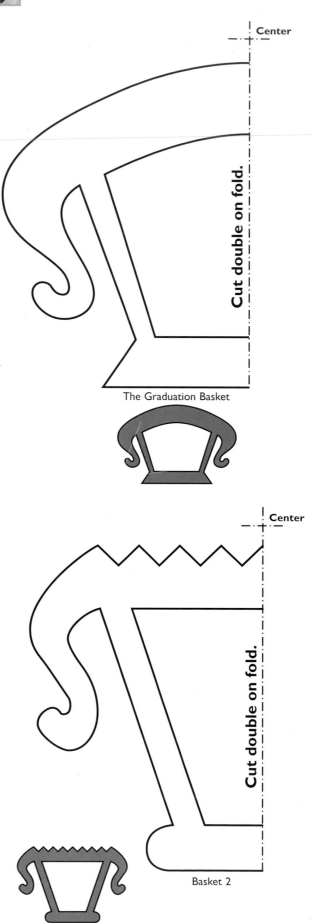

Center

Cut double on fold.

The Graduation Basket

Center

Cut double on fold.

Basket 2

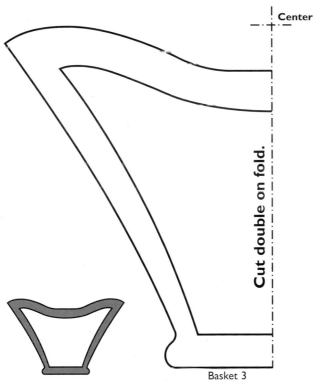

Center

Cut double on fold.

Basket 3

You've Now Graduated From These Lessons, Summa Cum Laude

Congratulations! Here's a Happy Graduation challenge.

Use two or more pattern elements from *Baltimore Elegance* to design and stitch a block using the Graduation Basket pattern from Lesson 6. Or, if you recognize these baskets as single-fold papercut designs from Lesson 4, design the whole block, basket included.

"For it is in using the coin of our times that our art has meaning for the future." I hope I get to see some of your sweet Albums.

Thank you. We've come to the end of our lessons. Some methods you've learned will have appealed, others will not. We're blessed to live in a time and a place in which we can learn all sorts of appliqué methods from each other. To have found love for a way of appliqué is a blessing. The first theme of this book is appliqué. The second theme is the joy of choices. The freedom to choose is a gift. You choose. For all God's children in appliqué, "Your way is the best way."

Thank you for choosing me to accompany you on this journey. From the bottom of my heart, thank you for your company.

Projects

The Grandmother Bag

"I will see you so soon, Ellie," I confided over the phone to my eldest grandchild, Eleanor Naomi, then just four. "I am coming to visit you, and we will read stories and draw and sew together."

"I am sewing right now, Grandma. I have to sew. My brother cut a hole in my blanket. So I have to fix it; I *have* to sew," she concluded a bit plaintively. I heard this as a charming duty-bound note, as though she were making the best of an unexpected but urgent chore in a day already full. She is her mother's little helper—folding clothes, ironing with her wooden iron, helping to empty the dishwasher and clear the table—so I understood her to be voicing the serious pretending whereby a child learns her adult role.

On a hot summer afternoon, New England–born Ellie had decided to call up a snowstorm.

When I arrived in Massachusetts, I gradually heard the other side of that story—a tale of creativity run amok. On a hot summer afternoon, New England–born Ellie had decided to call up a snowstorm. For starters, she knew where feathers—fine "fake snowflakes"—were. Snip! Snip! Snip! She plunged her small fist through the duvet cover's jagged cut and into her down comforter to pull out fistfuls of feathers. No silent snowstorm this, but one whirled and hurled with sibling shrieks of excitement! Ellie's mother, who had quickly come to see why all the noise, judged young Elias, just two, not dexterous enough to wield the scissors and figured Ellie was the perpetrator. Fantasy storm finished and lesson hopefully learned, Ellie—aided by Mama—whipped closed the comforter's hole against further loss. Knowing that the winter tale was painful to Ellie, I spoke not of it after I arrived, but sewed other things. I tailored a skirt that was too loose for her, hemmed a dress that was too long, sewed heart patches on a torn jumper.

When I visit my young grandchildren, I always bring my Grandmother Bag. In it I have art materials and other "making things"—a sandwich bag of 4″ quilt patches, small wrapped presents, my sewing apron, and my sewing case. I am reminded of myself at little Ellie's age and my summer family visits to Great Aunt Orpha and Great Uncle Bruce, down on the family farm in Mountain, West Virginia. At some point in our stay, we would drive to see Great Uncle Okey, the family doctor who lived with his wife, Great Aunt Elizabeth, in Charleston. He always had his worn black leather doctor's bag on hand. Whenever he visited with family, he would take out his stethoscope and listen to our hearts. Then he would look down our throats, into our eyes, and into our ears. Holding my Grandmother May Davina's wrist in a special way, he would take her pulse.

Recent photo with Elias age 3, Ellie age 5, and Davina age 2

Photo by Katja Sienkiewicz

I intend to be a visiting Grandma in the fashion of Great Uncle Okey—one who brings the tools of her trade when she visits so she can use them for the care of her family. Sometimes Grandpa and I baby-sit while mother or father, or both, go away for a retreat. Having a Grandmother Bag is second best to being in our own house: I know where things are in case of emergency!

During this particular visit, as was our custom, Ellie and I sometimes sat at the dining table, where the light is good for sewing. More often, we stitched in the morning, when all five of us—the three little ones, Grandpa (my husband, Stan), and I—walked 15 minutes downhill to McDonald's for breakfast. We had a happy routine— eating inside and then going into the small, well-worn play yard. The children loved to jump into the balls of the ball pit, burying them- selves amid the bouncing colors or carrying a few balls up to the bright yellow tunnel slide. At the top of the slide were two interior towers from which they could peer. "Hi, Grandpa," Elias would shout, waving. "Grandma, look at me!" Ellie called down to me.

My husband, born to Russian émigrés in flight from the Soviet Union, loves this, their chosen country, with a passion. When we look up to see our grandchildren in the McDonald's play-land tower, we can see a church steeple and an American flag fluttering atop its pole in the background. Almost every time we visit, my husband exclaims, with tears in his eyes, "This view is a wonderful, wonderful snapshot." I look down, smiling as I take another stitch, at peace.

I'm blessed with even more grandchildren now—and with happy recollections of those earlier Grandma stitching years: "Please," a then three-year-old Ellie beseeched me one day. "I love to sew so much. I don't get to sew a lot. Can I stitch color on something?"

"That's called embroidery," I explain. So we find a strand of perle cotton, and while I mend toes in tights, she embroiders her table napkin. When I hem a dress, she embroiders the same hem on the opposite side. I ask permission to cut those stitches so the hem will lie flat for ironing. She seems fascinated, but I don't push her by asking if I can pull them out. Not then. Not there. Her attention is rapt, but its span is not long. She wants to make a purse. I cut out a rectangle, pin and baste it, and then turn it right side out. She takes two stitches. I sew up the sides and make a buttonhole loop and show her how to do the buttonhole stitch over the loop to finish it. I ask her to hold the end of three 18″ strands of perle cotton so I can braid them. She turns and doesn't answer. A few minutes later she wanders back. "Do you want a hand-carrying handle, or do you want your purse to hang around your neck?" I inquire. "Around my neck," she chooses instantly. Then she proclaims, "It's a good thing you made it short so I can reach into it. And things won't fall out."

When the purse is finished, she puts money from her "store" into it, "so we can buy something," she says. Ellie shows the purse to her mother. "I made two stitches," she observes with pleasure, pointing. "These two stitches, right here."

You and I, Dear Reader, are stitchers. We love to sew. In a friend's kitchen or among strangers in an airport, this love uplifts. When we hold a cloth needle case handmade long ago, we smile, sensing the ancient sisterhood of stitching. Begin the projects with a pocket purse to stitch with a tiny child. Then go on to beautiful paraphernalia—regalia, really—for visiting stitchers, young and old!

Neck Purse

Made by Elly and Ellie

Finished size: 4¾″ × 5″

Embellishment: Fused heart or truck

*T*his is a great first sewing project for you and a three- or four-year-old, to get the feel and fun of our beloved craft.

If you are making this with a child, be sure to use small scissors with rounded points and a needle large enough for a child to grasp, such as a milliner's size #10. Avoid using a tightly woven fabric (such as a batik), which is difficult for children to stitch through.

Materials

- Fabric A: ¼ yard for neck pocket
- Fabric B: Scraps for fused embellishment
- 1 skein 6-strand embroidery floss for handle
- 1 skein 6-strand embroidery floss for blanket-stitching the appliqué
- Paper-backed fusible web

Cutting

Fabric A

Cut 1 rectangle 6″ × 21″.

Floss

Cut 9 strands 21″ long.

Making the Neck Purse

Purse

Top

5″

7″

Bottom

1. Follow the manufacturer's instructions to fuse your selected motif centered 7″ from the top of the rectangle on the right side of the fabric.

2. Fold each end of the purse, wrong sides together, 5″ from each end, so they meet in the middle.

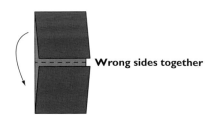

Wrong sides together

3. Fold the purse in half, right sides together, and pin twice on each side.

Right sides together

4. Use a ruler to draw a ½″ seam allowance on each long side of the purse.

5. Baste inside the seam allowance (not on the drawn line) and then remove the pins.

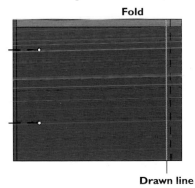

Fold

Drawn line

6. Start sewing the first few stitches on the drawn line, making sure the front and back align.

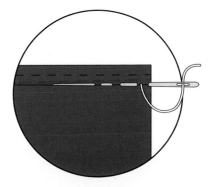

7. Show the child you're sewing with how to make the stitches and let him or her sew to the end of the seam. Secure the stitches. Knot the thread and sew the other side.

8. Turn the purse right side out and press.

Handle

1. Knot together the 9 lengths of floss. Try out the handle to see how much is needed to go around the neck. Allow for 1″ at each end to go inside the side seams of the purse.

2. Braid the needed length and tie a knot at the end.

3. Attach the braided handle by placing it 1″ from the top, over one side seam.

4. Fold the seam allowance over the braid and whipstitch the seam over the braid, securing it in the process. Repeat on the other side.

Finishing

1. Blanket-stitch the fused motif with a strand of floss.

2. On the back of the purse, write who made the purse and the year.

3. Fill with treasures.

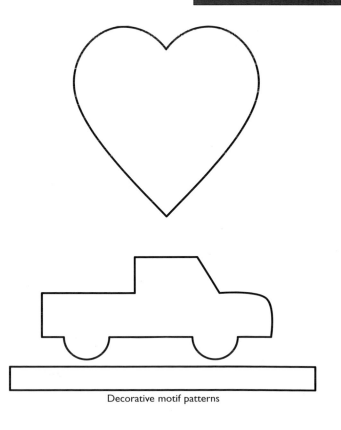

Decorative motif patterns

Grandmother and Granddaughter Sewing Aprons

Because I am almost always visiting, rather than being visited, I bring my sewing apron so I can stay mobile, with hands quickly freed to lift a crying babe if need be.

A sewing apron is a special gift for someone special. This is an easy project to share your love of appliqué with a child. Any small appliqué motif will look lovely.

Designed and made by Janice Vaine

Embellishment: Spun Rose (page 121) and Rose of Sharon (page 128)

Fabric requirements and instructions for grandchild's apron are noted in brackets.

Materials

- Fabric A: 1 yard [⅝ yard] for apron
- Fabric B: ⅝ yard [½ yard] for binding
- Scraps for appliqué embellishment

Cutting

Fabric A

Cut 1 rectangle 25″ × 33″ [16″ × 27″].

Trim out armholes following the measurements on the diagram.

Fabric B

Use a 1″ [¾″] bias tape maker to make 110″ [92″] of bias binding.

Making the Apron

1. Press the bottom edge up 8″ [6½″] for the pocket. Fold under the top edge ½″ twice and hem.
2. Appliqué on the right side of the pocket.
3. Turn under ½″ on the side edges of the apron and topstitch ⅜″ and ¼″ from the fold.
4. Stitch 2 [1] pocket divisions, 8″ [7½″] in from the side edges.
5. Bind the top edge of the apron.
6. Leave 25″ [22″] for the first tie. Bind the first armhole, leaving 21″ [18½″] binding free for the neck. Bind the second armhole, leaving 25″ [22″] for the second tie.
7. Appliqué the top of the apron.

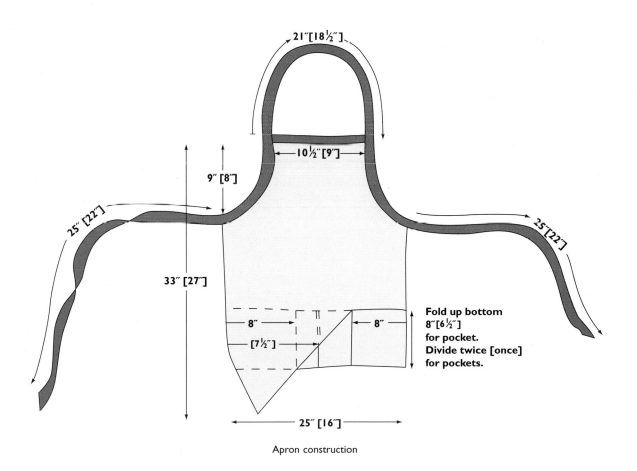

Apron construction

Sewing Case

Designed and made by Janice Vaine

Finished size: 8½″ × 17″ (open),
8½″ × 6″ (closed)

Embellishment: Ruched Rose
(page 81)

*M*y own simple sewing case, a gift from a fellow quilter, was the inspiration for this project. When Ellie was six, she was also so inspired and whipped up a twofold case with the sides stitched together from a rectangle of hot pink craft felt.

Materials

- Fabric A: Fat quarter for outside of case and binding
- Fabric B: ½ yard for lining and pockets
- Felted wool: 5″ × 6″ for needle case
- Hook-and-loop fastener: 1″ × 1″
- ⅜″ elastic: 23″
- Batting: 9″ × 17½″
- Button or small scrap of fabric for ruched flower

Cutting

Fabric A

Cut 1 rectangle 9″ × 17½″ for the case.

Cut 3 strips 2¼″ × 22″ for the binding. Sew together end to end.

Fabric B

Cut 1 rectangle 9″ × 17½″ for the lining.

Cut 1 rectangle 8½″ × 12″ for Pocket B.

Cut 1 rectangle 8½″ × 10″ for Pocket C.

Cut 1 rectangle 8″ × 9½″ for Pocket D.

Making the Sewing Case

Case

1. Layer the outside, batting, and lining. Quilt as desired. Trim to 8½" × 17".
2. Fold up the bottom of the case 5¾". Press.
3. Fold down the top of the case 5". Press. This forms Sections A, B, and C.
4. Round the top corners of Section A.
5. Sew a square of hook and loop fastener on the lining of Section A. Close the case along the fold lines and position another square of hook-and-loop fastener on the outside of Section C. Sew in place.
6. Fold the felted wool in half, forming a 3" × 5" needle case. Press.
7. Embellish the front and inside of the needle case as desired.
8. Center the needle case on the lining in Section A. Blindstitch in place, making sure the stitches do not show on the right side of the case.

Pocket B

1. Fold the 8½" × 12" pocket piece in half, forming an 8½" × 6" rectangle. Press.
2. Topstitch ¼" and ⅝" from the fold.
3. Cut a piece of ⅜" elastic 7½" long. Thread the elastic through the casing formed by the top stitching, securing it at each end.
4. Mark a line ⅜" above the bottom fold line of the case.
5. Place the raw edges of Pocket B along the marked line with the folded edge toward the bottom of the sewing case. Stitch ¼" from the raw edge. Press up and pin the sides in place.

Pocket C

1. Fold the 8½" × 10" pocket piece in half, forming an 8½" × 5" rectangle. Press.
2. Topstitch ¼" and ⅝" from the fold.
3. Cut a piece of ⅜" elastic to 7½". Thread the elastic through the casing formed by the topstitching, securing it at each end.

Pocket D

1. Fold the 8" × 9½" pocket piece in half, forming a 4" × 9½" rectangle. Press.
2. Topstitch ¼" and ⅝" from the fold.
3. Cut a piece of ⅜" elastic to 7½". Thread the elastic through the casing formed by the topstitching, securing it at each end.
4. Make 2 tiny pleats on the bottom of the pocket, bringing the width of Pocket D to 8½".
5. Draw a line down the center of Pocket D.
6. Place Pocket D on top of Pocket C, matching the bottom and side edges. Stitch down the marked center line on Pocket D.
7. Place Pocket C/D on the bottom of the case lining and pin it in place.

Finishing

1. Sew binding all around the case.
2. Sew a button or a ruched flower on the outside top flap, covering the stitching of the hook-and-loop fastener. Enjoy!

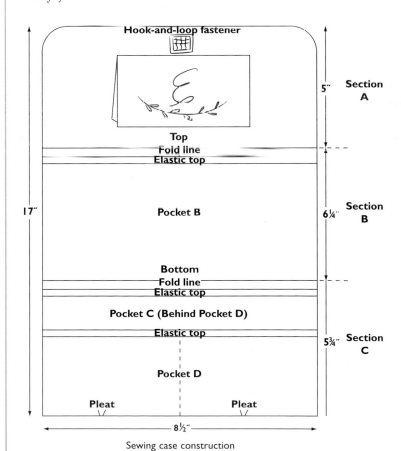

Sewing case construction

Grandmother and Granddaughter Totes

Designed and made by Janice Vaine

Finished sizes

Grandmother Tote: 15″ × 13½″ × 6″

Granddaughter Tote: 10″ × 9½″ × 4″

Embellishment: Rose of Sharon Bud (page 128)

*F*or materials and mending on a grandmother visit, the sewing tote made for me by Maryann McFee is so handy. With my sewing doll attached, it inspired this project. Watching you stitch with accoutrements like these would make any little person long to sew.

Note Fabric requirements and instructions for grandchild's tote are noted in brackets.

Materials

- Fabric A: 1¼ yards [¾ yard] for the outside of the tote
- Fabric B: 1¼ yards [¾ yard] for the lining
- Batting: ¾ yard [½ yard]
- 1¼″ [1″] cotton belting: 2 yards [1⅓ yards] for handles
- Foam-core board: 6″ × 15″ [4″ × 10″] for tote bottom

Cutting

Fabric A

Cut 2 rectangles 19″ × 23″ [14″ × 16″] for the front and back of the tote.

Cut 2 rectangles 8½″ × 10½″ [6″ × 8″] for the front pocket.

Fabric B

Cut 2 rectangles 18″ × 22″ [13″ × 15″] for the front and back lining.

Cut 2 rectangles 7½″ × 19½″ [5½″ × 14½″] for the bottom sleeve.

Batting

Cut 2 rectangles 19″ × 23″ [14″ × 16″] for the front and back of the tote.

Cut 1 square 8½″ × 8½″ [6″ × 6½″] for the pocket.

Making the Tote

Note All seam allowances are ½" unless otherwise noted.

Tote

1. Quilt the front and back sections as desired with the outer tote fabric and just the batting, not the lining.
2. Trim to 18" × 22" [13" × 15"].
3. Cut a 3" × 3" [2" × 2"] square from the bottom corners. Set aside.

Front Pocket

1. Place the pocket pieces right sides together with the batting on top. The batting will be 2" [1½"] shorter on the top of the pocket.
2. On both sides of the bottom edge, mark 1" [¾"] out from corner. Draw a diagonal line connecting the marks. Trim along this line.
3. Sew both sides, the corners, and the bottom edge with a ¼" seam allowance. Trim the batting close to the stitching, turn, and press.
4. Quilt and embellish as desired.
5. Turn down the top edge 1" [¾"], then again another 1" [¾"]. Press and hem.
6. Place the pocket on the right side of the quilted front piece, 3½" [2½"] from the top and 7" [4¾"] in from each side.
7. Edge stitch around the sides and bottom of the pocket to hold it in place.

Outside

1. Place the tote front and back pieces right sides together. Sew the side and bottom seams and press the seams open.
2. Pinch the bottom corners together, matching side seam to bottom seam. Pin and stitch, then turn the tote right side out.
3. Cut 2 handles 32" [24"] long from the belting. *Optional:* Stitch a decorative stitch down the middle of each handle.
4. Place a handle on the front and another on the back, both 6" [3½"] from each side edge. Pin and baste in place.

Lining

1. Place the lining front and back right sides together. Sew the side and bottom seams, leaving a 9" [6"] opening in the middle of the bottom seam for turning the bag later. Press the seams open.
2. Pinch the bottom corners together, matching side seam to bottom seam. Pin and stitch.

Putting It All Together

1. Place the tote into the lining, with right sides together and side seams matching.
2. Pin and stitch around the top edge. Turn through the opening in the bottom of the lining.
3. Press the top edge, rolling the lining fabric slightly to the inside. Topstitch around the top, ⅜" from the edge.
4. Sew the opening in the bottom of the lining closed.
5. Stitch 2 long sides and 1 short side of the sleeve pieces, right sides together. Turn the sleeve right side out.
6. Insert the foam-core board, turn the open edge to the inside, and place it in the bottom of the tote.

Off to Grandma's we go!

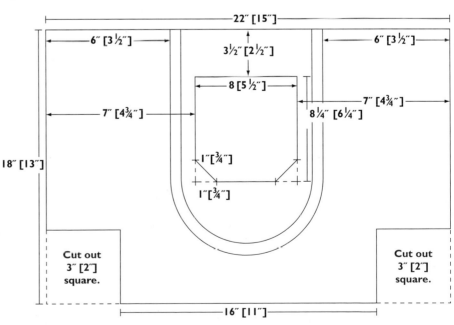

Tote construction

Babushka Sewing Doll

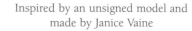

Inspired by an unsigned model and
made by Janice Vaine

Finished sizes
Grandmother's Babushka Doll: 4″ × 6″

Granddaughter's Babushka Doll: 3″ × 4½″

*T*he original doll had a Middle Eastern
look, with a traditional black-and-white
head scarf. Designed by Janice to look more
"Sienkiewicz," our sewing friend has the
look of a babushka (Russian for "old lady" or
"grandmother"). Who among us would not
love such a friend?

Note Fabric requirements and instructions for grandchild's babushka doll are noted in brackets.

Materials

- Fabric A: Fat eighth [9″ × 11″] for body
- Fabric B: 6″ × 6″ for apron
- Fabric C: ⅛ yard for scarf
- Flesh-colored fabric: 5″ × 5″ for face and hands
- Fusible web: 2¼″ × 4¾″ piece of Heat 'n' Bond or fusible webbing of choice
- 6-strand floss: Colors for facial features
- 6-strand floss: Braided cord
- Polyfil stuffing
- Play sand: ½ cup [¼ cup]
- Freezer paper
- Hot glue gun (or fabric/tacky glue)
- Small (doll-size) spool of thread
- Small (doll-size) scissors

Cutting

Patterns are on page 108.

Trace the following pieces onto the freezer paper, making sure to mark all pertinent points as indicated on the pattern: body, circle with facial features, hands, and apron.

Fold the flesh-colored cotton in half, wrong sides together. Press. Insert fusible webbing against the fold and fuse together. Cut 2 bodies, 2 aprons, 1 face, 1 right hand, and 1 left hand. Cut scarf fabric 4″ × 22″ [2½″ × 21″].

Making the Babushka Doll

Note All seam allowances are ¼″ unless otherwise noted.

Braided Cord

1. Cut 9 lengths of 6-strand floss 55″ [30″].
2. Knot the 9 lengths together with a slip knot at one end. Divide the floss into 3 units and braid. Knot at the end. You will use approximately 45″ [20″] for the doll.
3. Attach an end of the floss braid at the top of the back body piece, sewing back and forth over the braided cord to secure it at the seamline.

Face

1. Trace the facial features on the cut out face. Use a lightbox if necessary.
2. Use a strand of floss to embroider the facial features.
3. Use 2–3 strands of floss to embroider the hair with legged French knots (see page 106).
4. Use 9 lengths of 6-strand floss 22″ [12″] to make the braids. Divide the 9 lengths in half and stitch the center to the center of the top of the face. Measure down 1″ on both sides, tie at this point, and begin braiding. Braid to the desired length, tie with a bow, and trim the remaining floss. Set aside.

Apron Pocket

1. Sew 2 apron pieces right sides together. Stitch around the apron, leaving an opening between Points 1 and 2. Turn, press, and whipstitch the opening closed.
2. Use a decorative stitch on your sewing machine to stitch around the apron ¼″ from the edge.
3. Stitch the apron to the body front along the sides and bottom, following the placement on the pattern.

Body

1. Wrap the braided cord in a circle and place it in the center of the body back, so it will be out of the way.
2. Place the body front and back right sides together and stitch together, leaving an opening between Points 3 and 4. Turn right side out.
3. Place ½ cup [¼ cup] of play sand in the bottom of the doll.
4. Stuff the rest of the body with Polyfil. Whipstitch the opening closed.
5. Position the face on the body front, following the pattern placement. Hot glue in place.
6. Position the hands at the sides of the apron pocket, following the pattern placement. Hot glue in place.

Scarf

1. Wrap the scarf around the doll. Begin at the side of the face (just above the apron pocket), wrap around the top, around the other side of the face, across the front, around the back, twist 2 or 3 times, cross over the front above the apron pocket, and around to the back. Pin as necessary for a pleasing effect that drapes around the face and back.

2. Allow the scarf to self-press into shape overnight. The next day, gently unwrap the scarf and hot glue it to keep it in place at the beginning, around the face, at the top, over the hands, and at the end.

Scissors and Thread

1. Place a small thread spool in the apron pocket.
2. Tie the end of the braided cord to the little scissors and place them between the twisted part of the scarf and into the thread spool.

You can mold the sand in the bottom of the babushka doll so that the doll stands on a table. This doll also makes a lovely addition to your sewing tote, as shown on page 102.

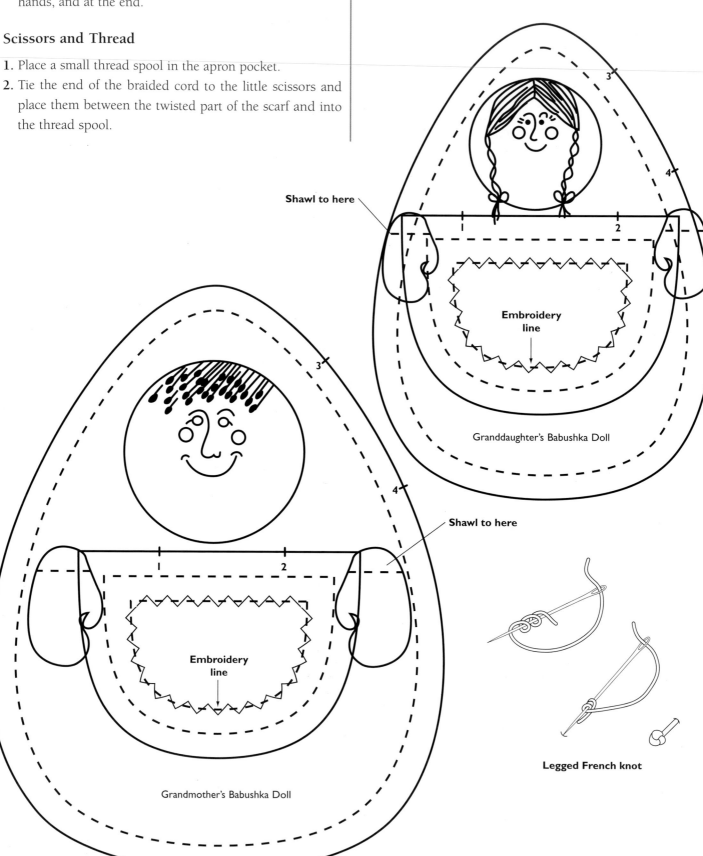

Shawl to here

Embroidery line

Granddaughter's Babushka Doll

Shawl to here

Embroidery line

Grandmother's Babushka Doll

Legged French knot

Baltimore Elegance Pillows

Designed and made by Janice Vaine

Finished size: 16½″ × 12½″

Embellishments. *Baltimore Elegance* blocks
(pages 121–149)

These pillows are quick to make, so you can make one for each new child in the family. Janice made one for each of my grandchildren: Colter Meadows, Severn Clare, Eleanor Naomi, Elias Emerson, Davina Teresa, and Jana Sophia. Thank you so much, Janice!

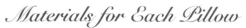

Materials for Each Pillow

- Fabrics A, B, C: 3 coordinating fat quarters for pillow front
- Fabric D: ½ yard for pillow back
- Fabric C: Fat quarter for binding (optional)
- Scraps for appliqué
- Pillow form: 16″ × 12″

Cutting for Each Pillow

Fabric A

Cut 1 rectangle 13½″ × 11½″ for the appliqué background.

Fabric B

Cut 1 rectangle 12½″ × 4″ for the bottom panel.

Fabric C

Cut 1 rectangle 6″ × 13½″ for the side panel.

Fabric D

Cut 2 rectangles 14″ × 13½″ for the pillow back.

Binding (optional)

Cut 4 strips 2″ × 22″, or enough bias strips for 80″.

Making the Pillow

Note All seam allowances are ½″ unless otherwise noted.

Pillow Front

1. Select an appliqué design and appliqué it onto Piece A. Trim to 12½″ × 10½″.
2. Sew the bottom panel (B) to the appliquéd panel (A).
3. Sew the left panel (C) to the left side of A/B.
4. Add embellishments (buttons, beads, additional appliqué, hand or machine embroidery) as desired.

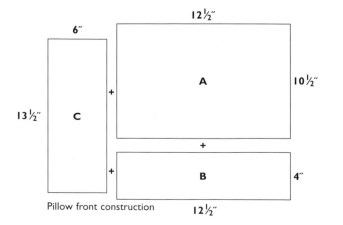

Pillow front construction

Pillow Back

1. On each back piece, fold under a 13½″ side 1¾″ two times. Press and then topstitch 1½″ from the folded edge.
2. Place the 2 back pieces on top of the pillow front, right sides together. Match the raw edges and overlap the topstitched folded edges in the center, forming a 17½″ × 13½″ rectangle.
3. Pin the back and front together. Stitch. Trim the corners, turn, and press.

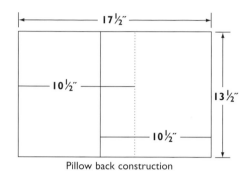

Pillow back construction

Binding (Optional)

1. Join the four 2″ × 22″ strips together end to end. Press them in half lengthwise, right sides together, to make approximately 80″ of binding.
2. Bind the pillow with a scant ¼″ binding to give the effect of piping around the pillow edge.

   Place the pillow form in the pillowcase and enjoy!

Album Block Carrying Case

Based on Joanne Maddelena's original design in *Papercuts and Plenty*; adapted and made by Janice Vaine

Finished size: 18″ × 18″ × 1½″

Embellishment: Wife, Mother, Sister, Daughter, Aunt (page 136)

Here's the perfect way to transport your Album blocks in style. The larger outside case fits the standard 12½″ × 12½″ Baltimore blocks, while the smaller size on the back of the carrier is perfect for your smaller (8″ × 8″) Baltimore blocks.

Of course, you can use this stylish block case for any of your blocks-in-progress.

Materials

- Foam core board: 2 squares 18″ × 18″, 1 rectangle 6½″ × 18″
- Fabric A: 1⅓ yards for the outside of the case
- Fabric B: 1⅓ yards for the case lining
- Fabric C: ½ yard for the ties and handle
- Thin batting: 1¾″ × 9″
- ⅝″ bias bar

Cutting

For the Larger Block Case

Fabric A

Cut 1 rectangle 18½″ × 46″ for the outside.

Cut 2 rectangles 6½″ × 18½″ for the flaps.

Fabric B

Cut 1 rectangle 18½″ × 46″ for the lining.

Cut 2 rectangles 6½″ × 18½″ for the flaps.

Fabric C

Cut 2 strips 1¼″ × 26″ for the ties.

Cut 1 strip 9″ × 1¾″ for the case handle.

For the Smaller Block Case

Fabric B

Cut 1 rectangle 10½″ × 24½″ for the lining.

Cut 2 rectangles 4½″ × 10½″ for the flaps.

Fabric C

Cut 1 rectangle 10½″ × 24½″ for the outside.

Cut 2 rectangles 4½″ × 10½″ for the flaps.

Cut 1 strip 1¼″ × 22″ for the ties.

Making the Album Block Carrying Case

Note All seam allowances are ¼″ unless otherwise noted.

Small Block Case

SIDE FLAPS

1. Place the 2 sets of 4½″ × 10½″ rectangles right sides together (1 Fabric C and 1 Fabric B per set).

2. Stitch around 2 short sides and a long side. Clip the corners, turn, press, and edge-stitch around the finished edges.

3. Pin the flaps to the long side of the outside piece of the smaller case (Fabric C), right sides together and 4¼″ from the top of the case. Baste in place. (See Figure A on page 113.)

TIES

1. Fold the 1¼″ × 22″ strip lengthwise, right sides together, and stitch. Turn right side out and press. Cut the tie in half to make 2 ties each 11″ long.

2. Baste a tie along the top flap, centered on the outside of the case.

3. For the remaining tie, fold under ½″ and pin 5″ from the outside bottom edge of the smaller case, centered between the sides.

4. Stitch the ties to the case by sewing a ¼″ × ¼″ square over the folded ends. Be sure both tie ends are pointed toward the bottom edge. (See Figure A.)

MAKING THE SMALL BLOCK CASE

1. Place the outside piece (with the flaps sewn on) and the small block case lining right sides together.

2. Pin the pieces together, being careful to tuck inside the ties and flaps.

3. Use a cup (or some other round shape) to round the corners at the top edge.

4. Stitch around all 4 sides, leaving a 6″ opening at the bottom edge for turning.

5. Trim the corners, turn, press, and edge-stitch around the finished edges. Set this aside.

Large Block Case

SIDE FLAPS

1. Place the 2 sets of 6½″ × 18½″ rectangles right sides together (1 Fabric A and 1 Fabric B per set).

2. Stitch around 2 short sides and a long side. Trim the corners, turn, press, and edge-stitch around the finished edges.

3. Pin the flaps to the long side of the outside piece of the Baltimore Album case (Fabric A), right sides together and 9″ from the top flap. Baste in place. (See Figure B on page 113.)

TIES

1. Fold both 1¼″ × 26″ strips lengthwise, right sides together, and stitch. Turn right side out and press. Cut the ties in half to make 4 ties each 13″ long.

2. Baste 2 ties along the top flap (6″ in from each side so that they are centered on the case).

3. On the remaining 2 ties, fold under ½″ and pin 11½″ from the front edge and 6″ from the side.

4. Be sure that the ends of the 4 ties are pointed toward the bottom edge, as in Figure B. Stitch the bottom ties by sewing a ¼″ × ¼″ square over the folded ends.

HANDLES

1. Cut a piece of thin batting 1¾″ × 9″. Place it on the wrong side of the 1¾″ × 9″ handle piece.

2. Fold the strip in half lengthwise, right sides together, and stitch ⅝″ from the fold.

3. Trim the batting close to the stitching. Turn and press with a bias bar, centering the seam in the middle. Edge-stitch both sides.

4. Turn under ¾″ on each end of the handle.

5. Pin the handle in place, 8″ from the top and 6″ in from each end (see Figure B). Stitch in place by sewing a ¼″ × ¾″ rectangle over each folded end.

Putting the Cases Together

1. Fold in the side flaps of the smaller block case, bottom edge up and top flap down to form a 10″ × 10″ square.

2. With the right side of the larger block case facing up and the flaps opened out, center the closed, smaller block case on the back of the larger block case, 4″ in from each side and 12⅞″ down from the top flap (see Figure A).

3. Carefully open the smaller block case and pin in place.

4. Stitch to the back around the inside to form a 9½″ × 9½″ square. Fold the smaller block case closed.

Finishing

1. Place the outside piece of the larger block case (with the flaps sewn on) and the lining right sides together.

2. Pin 2 long sides and the top (where the ties are). Make sure you tuck in the ties and flaps. Stitch around the 3 sides.

3. Trim the corners, turn, press, and edge-stitch to close the finished edges.

4. Insert the 6½″ × 18″ piece of foam core and stitch Line A (see Figure B) along the edge of the board (a zipper foot works well here).

5. Stitch Line B ⅞″ below the previous line of stitching to form the top flap and top.

6. Insert an 18″ × 18″ square of foam core and stitch along the edge (Line C). Stitch Line D ⅞″ below Line C to form the back and bottom.

7. Insert the other 18″ × 18″ square of foam core. Turn the remaining seam allowance inside (trim if necessary) and edge-stitch closed.

8. Close the case and tie it shut. Trim the ties to your desired length.

9. Embellish with your favorite *Baltimore Elegance* block

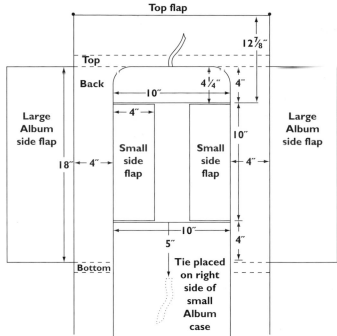

Figure A: Small Album block carrying case construction

May your Baltimore Album case become filled with the pleasures of your work.

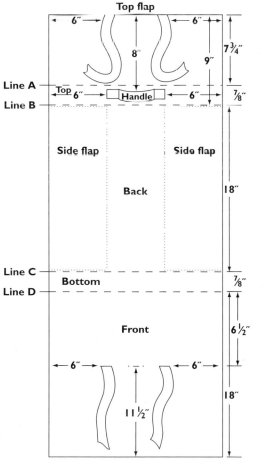

Figure B: Large Album block carrying case construction

How to Take a Pattern From the Book

Appliqué block pattern—*Appliqué (decorative shapes) in a predesigned arrangement for a quilt square. The vertical and horizontal centers drawn on the pattern allow you to transfer its arrangement to a square (of paper or fabric) with the same lines creased into it. Various ways to transfer the shapes (and their placement) from the book to the fabric are taught below. In general, to transfer the pattern from the book, the shapes—to keep their size—should be cut out precisely on their printed or traced lines.*

Papercut appliqué pattern—*A block pattern cut from a folded square of paper. Papercuts are frequent patterns in my Baltimore Beauties books. The simplest fold is in half—for example, the familiar heart-shaped pattern. The most common papercuts are cut from paper folded into eighths. The first five lessons of this book teach eight-layer papercut blocks. Because the different motifs are attached (snowflake-like), a special approach to appliqué—Cutaway by Needleturn (pages 22–23)—works particularly well for papercut patterns. Appliqué From the Back (pages 57–59), and Fused Appliqué (page 33), also work for appliquéing papercuts. Separate Unit Appliqué is sometimes combined with a papercut pattern.*

Separate unit appliqué pattern— *An appliqué block pattern made up entirely of separate units of appliqué. Lesson 6 focuses on Separate Unit Appliqué. By the time you reach that lesson, you will know that there are ways other than those taught in Lesson 6 to do the appliqué. To have learned the freedom to choose among them is to have become an appliquér! These separate motifs can be appliquéd by a Nonprepared Method (where you use Needleturn to turn under the seam allowance as you sew). Alternatively, use a Prepared Method (where the seam is preturned under and basted or glued or held in place by Freezer Paper Inside). Some patterns (like the one in Lesson 5) combine both papercuts and Separate Unit Appliqués. Some Separate Unit Appliqués can be adapted by Pattern Bridges (page 117) to make them suitable for Cutaway by Needleturn.*

Papercuts

To make a complete papercut pattern, follow the directions below.

1. Fold an 8″ × 8″ square of freezer paper (shiny side in) into 4 quadrants. Orient the square so that there is a fold on the left, 2 folds at the top, and raw edges at the right and bottom.

Fold into 4 quadrants.

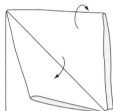

2. Fold down the upper right corners to the lower left corners—the front to the front, the back to the back.

Fold down upper corners.

3. You should have 3 folds on the left and 2 folds on the right. Mark the outside edge **E** and the center **C** on both top and bottom layers.

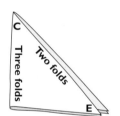

Note position of folds.

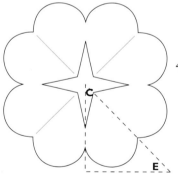

4. If you are making your own papercut (as in Lesson 4), draw your design on the top layer of this 8-layer triangle.

Draw design on top layer.

If you are copying a design from this book, unfold the freezer paper and place it shiny side down on the original pattern, orienting the pattern by matching the pattern fold lines and the center (**C**) and edge marks (**E**) to the freezer paper. Use repositionable tape to hold the paper in place over the pattern. Trace either an eighth or a quarter of the pattern.

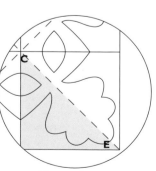

Trace pattern.

5. Fold the paper and staple inside the appliqué design to keep the layers from shifting. Use excellent paper scissors and cut off the drawn line (so that the pattern's inside corners don't grow, like a sugar cookie in the oven).

> *Note* Separate Unit Appliqué shapes should be cut out separately and set aside. An exception is Lesson 2: Back-Basted Appliqué, where both layers of the pattern are traced onto the background fabric.

Separate Unit Appliqués

- For Separate Unit Appliqué, you may need to trace or cut the patterns apart. For example, The Mother's hair template (page 136) needs to be traced off separately. If you choose to appliqué her cheeks (perhaps Ultrasuede) instead of doing them by ink or embroidery, then you'll need to create separate templates for those as well. And so forth.

- When a pattern is layered so that entire pattern motifs overlap, you'll need to trace those separate elements as separate templates (Note the overlapping leaves on the rose on the Lyre Wreath in Bloom, page 129.)

Enlargement Percentages for Larger Album Block Sizes

The patterns in this book are presented for an 8″ × 8″ finished block, as an introduction to the Baltimore Album style. You might enjoy it so much that you want to enlarge the patterns and go on to make full-size blocks and quilts in the classic Baltimore Album style.

You will also need to enlarge the reproduction blocks on pages 150–157. The simplest way is to use a photocopier to enlarge these blocks.

Current design area: 7″ on an 8½″ × 8½″ square (includes ¼″ seam allowance all around) makes an 8″ block, finished. The 12½″ unfinished block size is that of the *Baltimore Beauties* series.

For a 10″ finished block—Enlarge 129% (9″ design area).

For a 12″ finished block—Enlarge 165% (11½″ design area).

For a 13″ finished block—Enlarge 179% (12½″ design area).

For a 14″ finished block—Enlarge 186% (13″ design area).
For a 16″ finished block—Enlarge 215% (15″ design area).
For an 18″ finished block—Enlarge 243% (17″ design area).
For a 22″ finished block—Enlarge 300% (21″ design area).

You can also refer to page 174 for more books in the Baltimore Album series, where you'll find more lessons and classic patterns.

Pattern Transfer Methods

How you transfer a pattern depends on the type of pattern and the appliqué method. The seven methods described on the following pages describe how to transfer any type of appliqué pattern.

Method 1: Separate Unit Appliqué With a Drawn Turn Line
TO MAKE THE TEMPLATE

Trace the pattern onto the paper side of freezer paper, then cut out each shape. Don't add any seam allowance. Alternatively, you can photocopy the pattern onto page-size self-stick label sheets, available at office supply stores. Use these templates as you would the freezer paper.

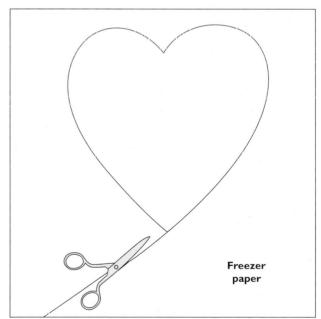

Freezer paper

Make freezer paper template.

TO USE THE TEMPLATE

1. Lightly iron a template onto the right side of the appliqué fabric.

2. Draw around the freezer-paper template with a Pigma .01 pen or other fabric-marking pen. I prefer a permanent pen that won't run when wet, such as the silver Sakura Gelly Roll, which marks both light and dark fabrics. This line is the turn line and is turned under to hide the mark.

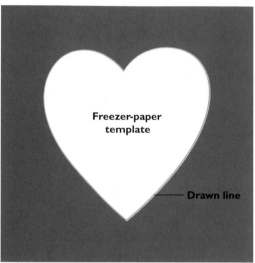

Draw around template.

3. Remove the freezer-paper template and cut out the appliqué, adding a $^3/_{16}"$ seam allowance beyond the drawn turn line.

Cut out adding $^3/_{16}"$.

4. Refer to Pin Placement on the next page, Pattern Veil (pages 118–119), marking the background (page 117 and 118), and using a lightbox (page 119) for methods of placing the appliqués on your block.

Method 2: Cutaway Appliqué With a Drawn Turn Line

Cutaway appliqué patterns are occasionally presented as a whole rather than as a fraction of the whole. When presented as a whole, photocopy it or trace it from the source. Place your pattern copy on a lightbox and trace the pattern onto the right side of the appliqué fabric.

More often, cutaway appliqués are designed and cut from folded paper (papercuts). Follow the directions on page 114 for making a complete papercut pattern on freezer paper. Follow the steps below to transfer the pattern to the appliqué fabric.

1. Cut the appliqué fabric into an 9″ × 9″ square. Finger-press the square lightly into quadrants to make it easier to center the pattern. Open up the square and place it right side up on the ironing board.

2. Place the freezer-paper template shiny side down on the right side of the appliqué fabric. Align the pattern's quadrant folds over the fabric's quadrant creases.

3. Use a hot, dry iron preheated to the cotton setting to iron the template lightly to the fabric.

4. Draw around the paper template with a Pigma .01 pen or other fabric-marking pen. I prefer a permanent pen that won't run when wet, such as the silver Sakura Gelly Roll, which marks both light and dark fabrics. Remove the paper template.

5. Prepare the block by pinning the pattern-marked appliqué fabric to the background (see Preparing a Block for Cutaway Appliqué, in Getting Started, page 23).

Prepare block.

Method 3: Cutaway Appliqué With Freezer Paper on Top

1. Make a full freezer-paper template. (See Papercuts on page 114.)

2. Work over a hard surface (cardboard or breadboard). Use a hot, dry iron preheated to a linen setting to iron the freezer-paper template tightly to the appliqué fabric. Lift the heel of the iron a bit so that you are pressing hardest on the tip of the iron. Push hard—especially at the pattern points and cut edges. (*Warning:* When ironing freezer paper to polished cotton, silk, or Ultrasuede, use a synthetic setting and a quick, light touch.)

3. Prepare the block for Cutaway Appliqué as described on page 23.

Note Temporary Pattern Bridges: Because I so loved Cutaway Appliqué With Freezer Paper on Top, I devised a way to even do separate units by cutaway. Simply cut temporary ¼"-wide paper bridges into the pattern to join (or bridge) the separate units. Cut off the bridges one at a time as you are ready to appliqué where the bridge touches. Try these pattern bridges in Lesson 5.

Method 4: Separate Unit Appliqué With Freezer Paper on Top

1. Trace the pattern onto the paper side of freezer paper. Cut out each shape. Don't add any seam allowance.

2. Work over a hard surface (cardboard or breadboard). Use a hot, dry iron preheated to a linen setting to iron the freezer paper template tightly to the appliqué fabric.

3. Pin this pattern-ironed-to-fabric to the background. Use at least 2 small appliqué pins (1 pin acts as a pivot) or else baste it. Now you're ready to needleturn.

First Aid for Too-Successful Adhesion

Once in a while, you might find you are a real a superwoman and have pressed the freezer paper to the fabric so successfully that the paper shreds when you attempt to pull off the template. Stop right there. Get tweezers. Iron to reheat (soften) the plastic coating on the freezer paper. Grab a solid cut edge (opposite the shredded paper) and pull back toward the shredded area to lift it up. It is rare for the paper to stick too well. Usually the story is one of frustration because the paper lifts. So this is our childhood Goldilocks lesson all over again, but applied to ironing— not too heavy, not too light, but just right!

Method 5: Marking the Background Fabric

1. Photocopy the pattern and place it right side up over a lightbox.

2. Center the background and pin it right side up on the pattern.

3. Use a fine pencil or permanent pen (Pigma or Gelly Roll Silver) to trace the pattern ¹⁄₁₆″ inside the printed appliqués onto the background. Iron to heat-set. When appliquéing, use Pin Placement to make sure the drawn line is covered.

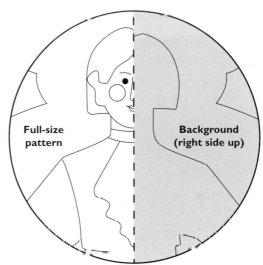

Trace pattern ¹⁄₁₆″ inside printed appliqué.

I prefer marking the right side of the background with the full pattern for complex separate unit appliqués, such as Husband, Father, Brother, Son, Uncle (page 137). I then do the appliqué shapes with the freezer-paper template ironed to the right side of the appliqué fabric and the seam allowance cut beyond it to be needleturned under. (If you don't like Freezer Paper on Top, you could simply draw the turn line and remove the freezer paper.)

MINIMAL MARKING AND PIN PLACEMENT FOR POSITIONING THE APPLIQUÉ

Minimal marking is a technique you can use if you don't enjoy the fixed attention required to make sure the Method 5 drawn line is always covered as you stitch. The goal is to make small recognizable marks that specify placement. Avoid something that looks like a confusing mass of dots and squiggles! Minimal marking is a bit like code or shorthand, and you can make up your own. For example, I use an X to mark the center of a circle when marking for grape appliqués. For leaves, I put a "<" ¹⁄₁₆″ inside each point and join the arrows by a straight line representing the center vein "<—>". Similarly, see the dots marking floral placement in Lesson 3 (page 64).

To make sure the appliqué is well placed, put a pin through the appliqué and through the marking into the background. See Lesson 3.

Method 6: Marking the Wrong Side of the Background

Use this technique for Appliqué From the Back (Lesson 2, page 57).

1. Finger-press the 9″ × 9″ background square into quarters to mark the vertical [a] and horizontal [b] centers. Place it wrong side up on the ironing board.

2. Make a freezer-paper template and center it over the **wrong side** of the background, guided by the crease lines. If the pattern has separate units or multiple appliqué layers (like Hearts and Leaves, page 134), cut off the separate units and other layers and save them for Step 4.

3. When marking the wrong side for appliqué, mark what will appear as the top layer first by drawing around the top layer of the freezer-paper pattern with a fine Pigma .01 black permanent pen [c].

4. If you've cut off any separate units, iron the cut-off shapes back in place [d]. Draw around them, and then remove all the paper templates. Heat set the ink.

5. Alternatively, use Method 5 (previous page), but mark the wrong side of the background.

Note If you are using a pattern shown as a whole and don't need to make a freezer-paper pattern, photocopy the pattern and place it right side up on a lightbox. Pin the paper and fabric layers together to keep alignment. Then simply trace the appliqué pattern onto the wrong side of the background square.

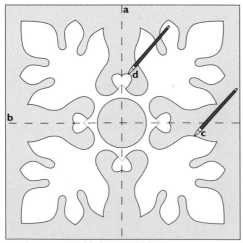

Mark wrong side.

Method 7: Pattern Veil

This is also called overlay or transparency appliqué. The pattern is printed or traced on a see-through material so that the appliqués can be moved into place on the background fabric, using the transparency as a guide. Lessons 5 (pages 78–79) and 6 (page 89) illustrate variations of this method. At its simplest, you can photocopy the pattern onto a clear transparency sheet. Office stores sell this material for overhead projector use. You can also trace the pattern onto a reclosable gallon plastic bag and use it to hold your unsewn appliqués as well. For patterns larger than 8½″ × 11″, use Quilter's Vinyl (see inside back cover), or use the kind of household plastic that is used for tablecloths. My favorite is to use a nonwoven product like PatternEase (available at fabric and quilting shops), when making the veil/transparency.

1. Photocopy the pattern and place it right side up over a lightbox.

2. Finger-press an 8″ × 8″ square of PatternEase into quarters. Open it up and pin it over the pattern, aligning its fold lines with those printed on the pattern.

3. Trace the pattern, using a Pigma .05 or a bold pen (like a fine Sharpie), onto the PatternEase square.

4. Use a gridded ruler to draw a basting line across the top of the square, ½″ down from the top.

5. Finger-press a 9″ × 9″ background square into quarters, then open it. Pin the pattern veil over it, aligning the folds [a]. You may have to restore the vertical and horizontal creased center lines to align them with those on the veil.

6. Use cotton or poly/cotton thread (not silk) to running stitch the drawn line [b] to hold the pattern veil to the background at the top of the square.

7. To use the veil, iron a freezer-paper template (for a Separate Unit Appliqué) to the right side of the appliqué fabric and cut it out, leaving a seam allowance beyond the paper. The freezer paper makes the appliqué shape (a leaf, for example) highly visible as you slip it under the veil. Pin the leaf appliqué to the underside of the veil. The white of the freezer paper will fill the leaf drawing; the seam allowance will show outside the leaf drawing. Now lower the veil to the background fabric.

8. Put another pin through the veil and the leaf template, pinning them to the background [c].

9. Carefully remove the first pins, freeing the veil. Lift the veil out of the way. Attach the appliqué to the background with more than one pin or baste so it does not shift [d]. This method is good for appliqués made of multiple separate units, like the flowers in Lesson 6 or Wife, Mother, Sister, Daughter, Aunt (page 136).

10. To make a line for a stem, lower the veil and put a Pigma pen through the porous PatternEase to mark the background directly with a dotted line. Or simply put the paper pattern on a lightbox. Align and pin the background over it, then trace the stem line.

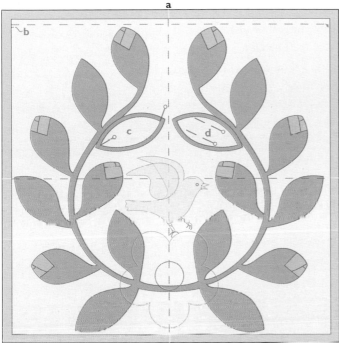

Using a marked pattern veil

Then let me to the valley go
This pretty flower to see
That I may also learn to grow
In sweet humility.

Additional Pattern Transfer Method

What pattern transfer method have we left out? How about placing a pattern over a lightbox, then returning to the lightbox as needed for pinning appliqué shapes in place. Or try using a lightbox to position and pin or glue-baste all the shapes in a block.

The world would be very silent if no birds sang there except those who sang best.

Patterns

Baltimore Elegance Blocks

Reproduction Blocks

Borders

Spun Rose

Symbolism

Roses—Love; Flower of Venus—Goddess of love

Vintage Inscription

God gave us memories
So that we may
Have roses in December

—James M. Barrie

Examples

See quilts on pages 36, 38, 40, 43, and 44.

Pattern Notes

See Lesson 3 (page 61) for inspiration on the flower treatment.

See Lesson 5 (page 75) for pattern bridges in putting down the greenery by Cutaway Appliqué.

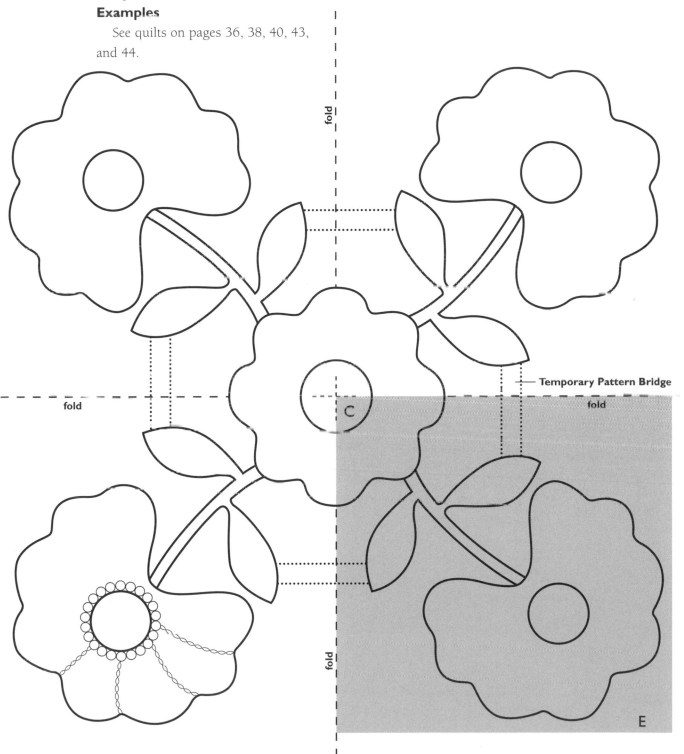

fold

fold

fold

fold

C

— **Temporary Pattern Bridge**

E

Crossed Flowers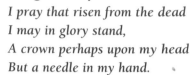

Symbolism

Cockscomb—Resurrection, dayspring

Vintage Inscription

I pray that risen from the dead
I may in glory stand,
A crown perhaps upon my head
But a needle in my hand.

—Antique needlework inscription

Examples

See quilts on pages 36, 37, 38, 40, 41 and 44.

Pattern Notes

This block is taught in Lesson 3.

Template pattern D is 1⅛″-diameter circle.

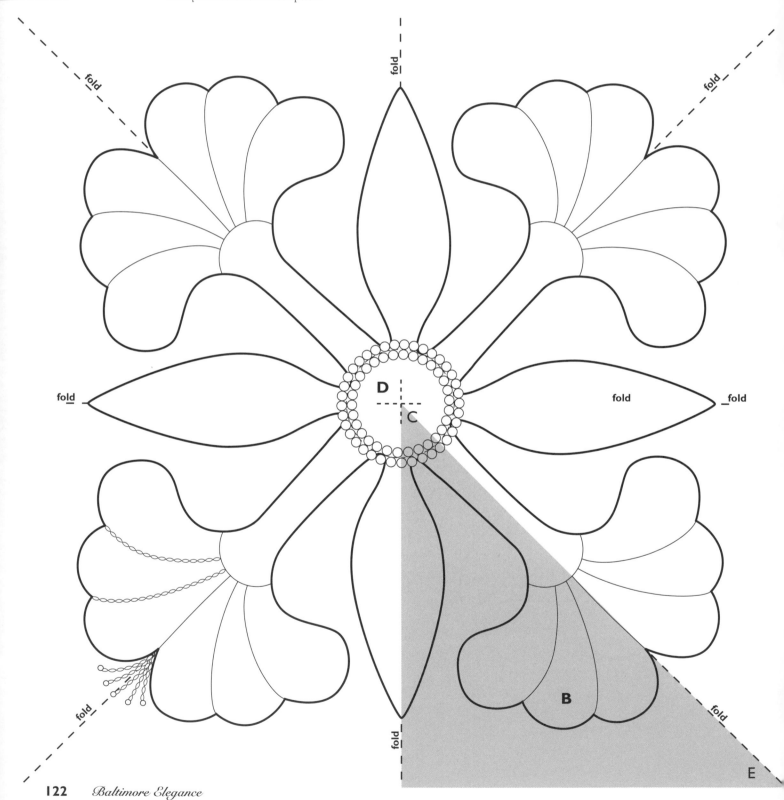

Spinning Ruched Roses

Symbolism

Roses—Love

Vintage Inscription

May this year's roses be
Many and sweet
And few be the thorns
Where wander thy feet.

—1893 needlework inscription

Examples

See quilts on pages 35, 39, and 42.

Pattern Notes

Mark the solid stem line only on the background.

Ruching is taught in Lesson 5, stems in Lesson 6, and the stem stitch in Lesson 1.

Ruched Hyacinth

Symbolism

Hyacinth—Peace of mind, prudence, yearning for heaven, unobtrusive loveliness

Vintage Inscription

Friendships multiply joys and divide griefs.

—Henry George Bohn

Examples

See quilts on pages 36, 38, 40, and 43.

Pattern Notes

1. The Ruched Hyacinth [B] is most easily done in ⅞″-wide French shaded wire-edged ribbon* (you'll need about 5″).

Shell ruche, 1″ from mountain peak to mountain peak (see Lesson 5, page 81). Needleturn the starting end of the ruched strip to the curve of the flowers drawn on the green. *Can substitute with 1″ × 5″ bias cotton.

2. Make 8 of the overleaf [C] from fusible-backed fabric. Fold one in half lengthwise. Iron it to itself. Appliqué its fold (from the dot down) over the flower and then appliqué its outside edge back up to the top of the leaf.

3. Draw shape [D] onto the appliqué. Fill it with colonial knots, then outline its shape with green outline stitch.

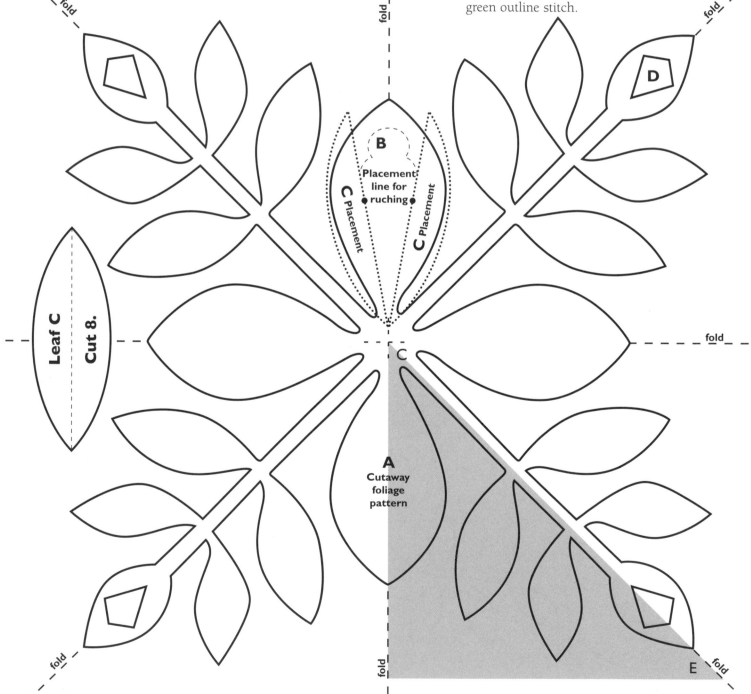

Rake Ruched Rose Wreath

Symbolism

Roses—Love; Flower of Venus—Goddess of love

Vintage Inscription

And every thought of you, a rose.

Examples

See quilts on pages 37 and 44.

Pattern Notes

1. Trace the wreath (including attached stems and leaves) onto the paper backing of fusible web. Follow the package directions for fusing greenery to the background. Blanket-stitch the edges with 1 strand of 6-strand embroidery floss (see page 33).

2. Machine sew the 2 leaves [A] right sides together. Slit the back and turn the leaf right side out. Attach to the block by running stitches through the center vein line.

3. Rake ruching and buds are taught in Lesson 5. The rake ruching can be done from a 1¼″ strip of bias fabric folded in half lengthwise.

4. Fill the center with Colonial knots made from 5 strands with 2 wraps (page 32).

Stem stitch

Above the dotted line, leave the calyxes unbonded until the bud has been inserted.

Use Template B (page 129) for the buds.

fold

Crown of Cherries

Symbolism

Cherries—Sweet character, good deeds

Vintage Inscription

That which cometh from the heart will go to the heart.

- Jeremiah Burroughes

Examples

See quilts on pages 37, 40, 41, 43, and 44.

Pattern Notes

Transfer the foliage pattern to fabric with pattern bridges, as in Lesson 5 (page 75).

Choose circle options from Lesson 6 (page 89).

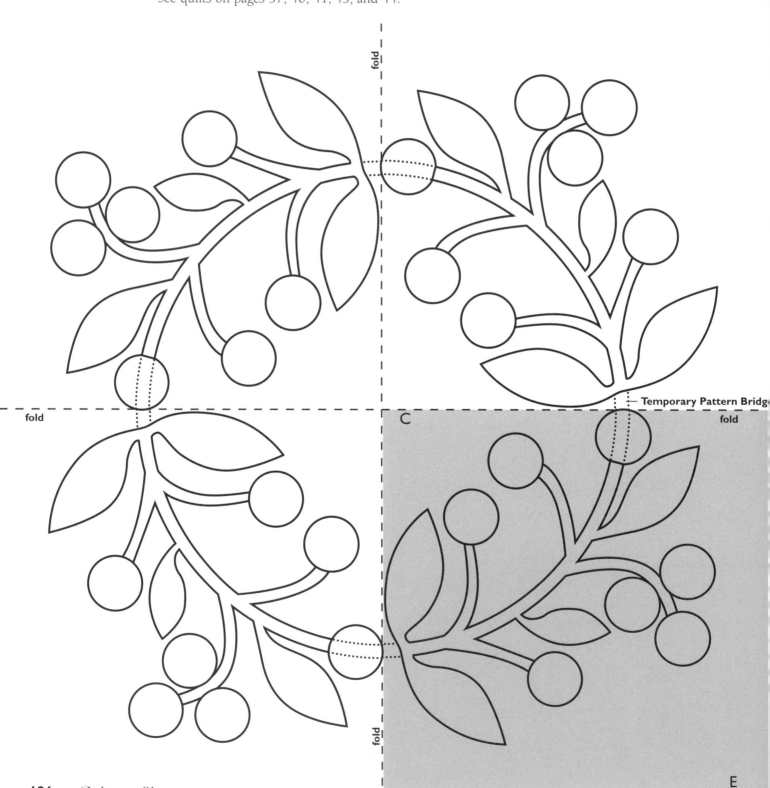

← **Temporary Pattern Bridge**

C

E

Red-Tipped Laurel Wreath

Symbolism

Laurel—Triumph, victory, eternity, success and renown, pride and good fortune

Vintage Inscription

Sweet Remembrance

Examples

See quilts on pages 38, 40, 41, 43, and 44.

Pattern Notes

Trace the right half of the pattern onto an 8″ × 8″ freezer-paper square folded in half. Cut double on the fold.

Use Cutaway Appliqué to do the stem and all but the top three leaves from one piece of green.

See Lesson 5 for Pattern Bridges in putting down the greenery by Cutaway Appliqué.

Traditionally the top three leaves and bow are red and are done using Separate Unit Appliqué.

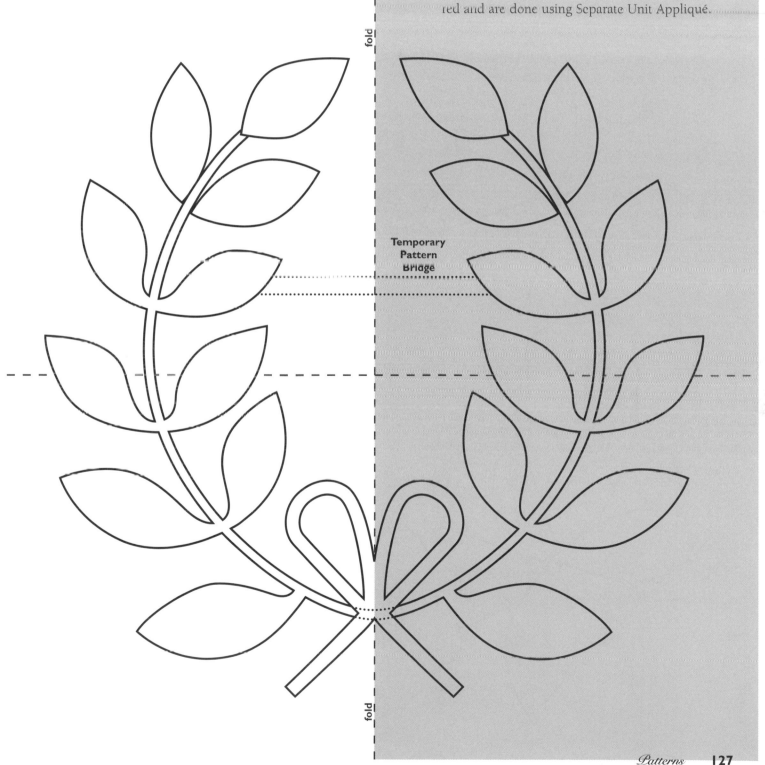

fold

Temporary
Pattern
Bridge

fold

Rose of Sharon

Symbolism

Rose of Sharon—Romantic love; linked with love from the Song of Solomon

Vintage Inscription

Pleasant words are like a honeycomb, sweetness to the soul and health to the body.

—Proverbs 16:24

Examples

See quilts on pages 36, 37, 40, 41, 43, and 44.

Pattern Notes

This pattern is taught in Lesson 6 (page 85).

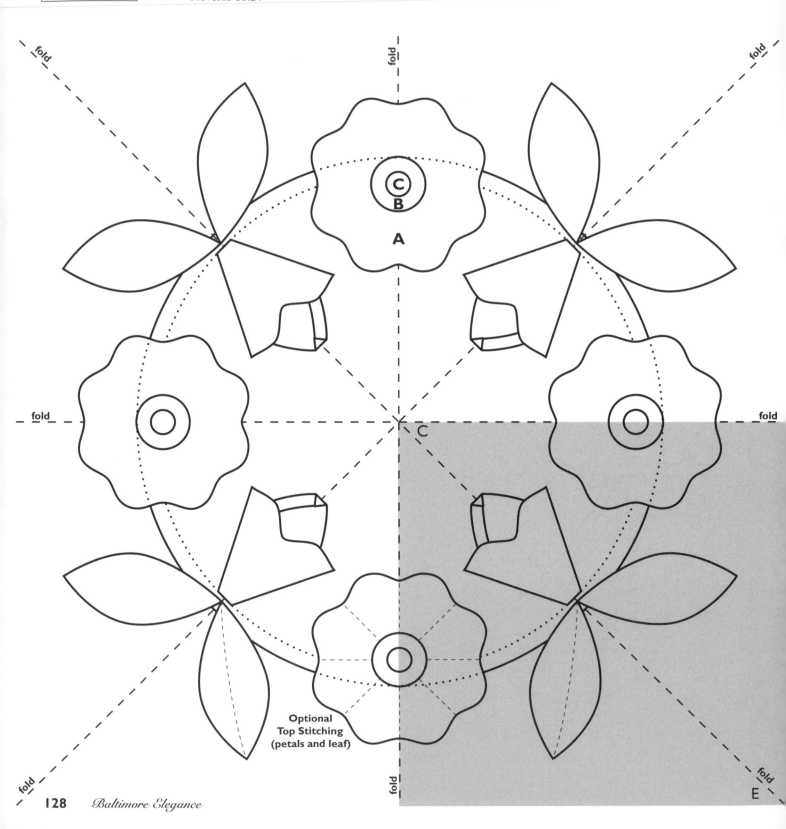

Optional
Top Stitching
(petals and leaf)

Lyre Wreath in Bloom

Symbolism

Lyre—All music in honor of God; Bird—Life of the soul; Rose—Love; Single rose—Simplicity; Rosebud—Beauty, purity, youth

Vintage Inscription

The world would be very silent if no birds sang there except those who sang best.

—John James Audubon

Contemporary inscription

Rejoice! Our Sweet Child is born!

Examples

See quilts on pages 36, 37, 39, 40, 41, 43, and 44.

Pattern Notes

1. Cut 1 Template A for the lyre wreath. (Cut double on the fold.)
2. Cut 8 circles from Template B for folded rosebuds
3. Cut 2 each of Template C, or cut 2 each of Templates Ca and Cb for split leaf option.
4. Cut 1 each of Template Da (bird body) and Db (separate wing). Appliqué the head, then draw the beak [Dc] to be satin stitched after appliqué.
5. Cut 1 Template E for the rose.
6. Cut 1 Template F (½″ diameter) circle for the rose center.

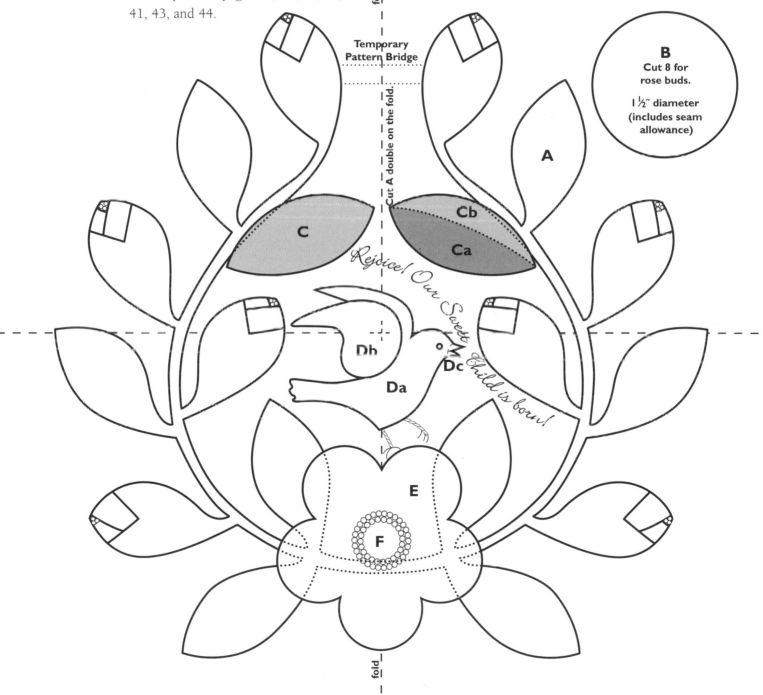

Crossed Stems With Yo-Yo Roses

Symbolism

Multiflora rose—Grace; Rosebud—Beauty, purity, youth

Vintage Inscription

As lonely through this world I stray,
And pass the pensive hours;
May truth and virtue point the way
And strew my path with flowers.

—M.E. Peach, Maryland, 1850

Examples

See quilts on pages 36, 39, 41, 42, and 44.

Pattern Notes

Trace the left half of the pattern onto an 8″ × 8″ freezer-paper square folded in half. Open the square up and delete Stem A from the right half.

See page 146 for instructions on making the Yo-yo Roses.

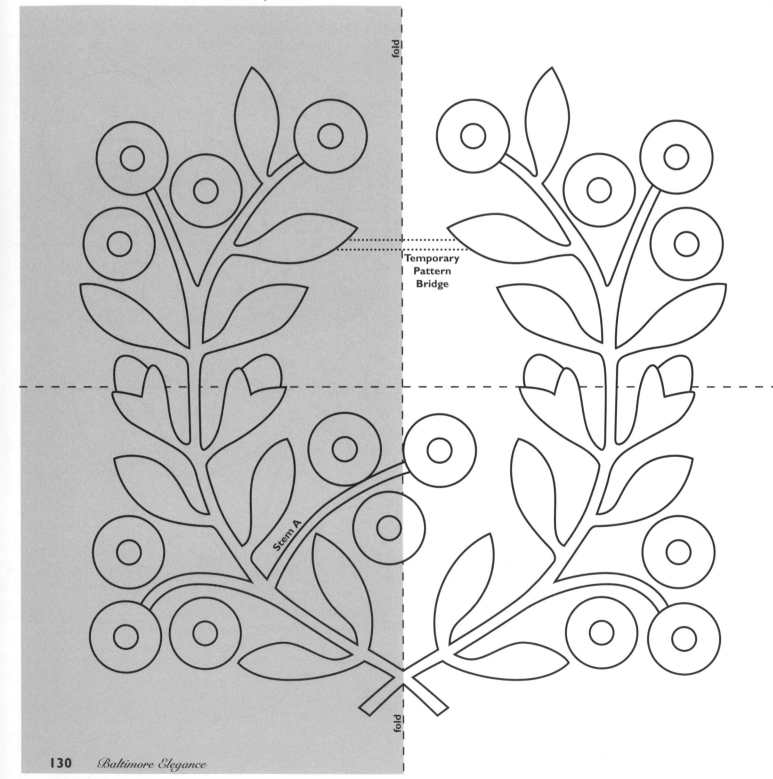

fold

Temporary
Pattern
Bridge

Stem A

fold

Wreathed Heart

Symbolism

Heart—Charity, love, piety, devotion

Vintage Inscription

Let health and happiness be thy lot,
All I ask is Forget me not.

—1849 needlework inscription

Examples

See quilts on pages 35, 36, 38, 40, 43, and 44.

fold

Temporary Pattern Bridges

fold

Patterns **131**

Ruched Rose Heart Wreath

Symbolism

Roses—Love

Vintage Inscription

Then let me to the valley go
This pretty flower to see
That I may also learn to grow
In sweet humility.

—1810 needlework inscription

Examples

See quilts on pages 35, 39, 40, 41, 43 and 44.

Pattern Notes

Ruching is taught in Lesson 5 (pages 81–82), stems in Lesson 6 (page 88).

The appliquéd stems can be pattern bridged in the manner of Lesson 5.

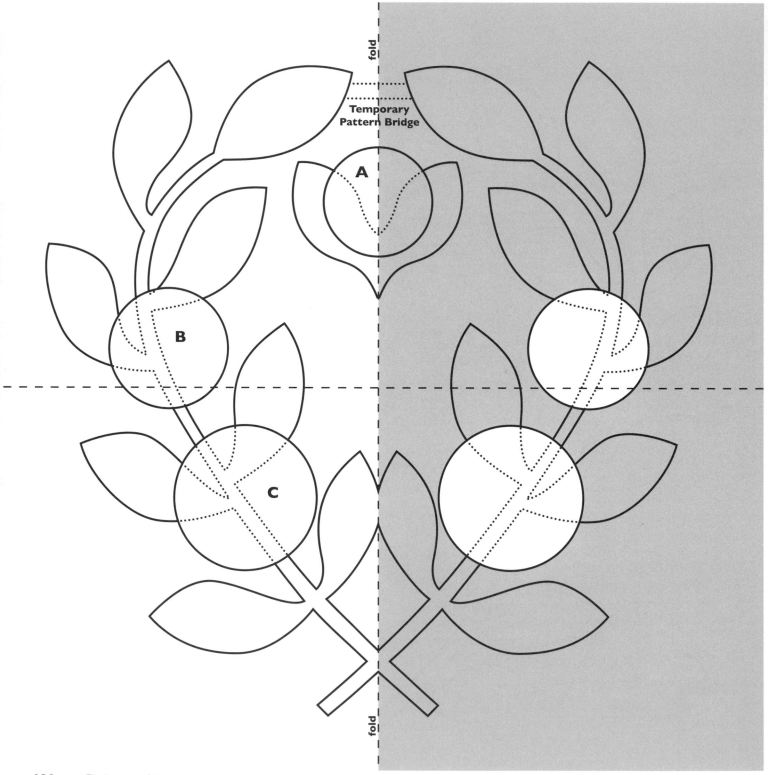

Tulip Wreath

(Inspired by Carol Wight Jones)

Symbolism

Heart—Love, devotion; Tulip—Renown, fame, spring, dreaminess

Vintage Inscription

To snatch the passing moment and examine it for eternity is the noblest of occupations.

—Louis J. Halle

Examples

See quilts on pages 36, 38, 40, 41, and 44.

Pattern Notes

See page 146 for Fringe and Fold Flower templates.

Do the tulips as flat appliqués or add some dimension like these Fringe and Fold Flowers.

1. Fringe the first ³⁄₁₆″ raw edge of Templates A and B.
2. Gluestick the center of Circle B to Circle A, right sides up.
3. Fold into quarters, with the smaller circle on the outside.
4. Tuck into the tulip calyx.

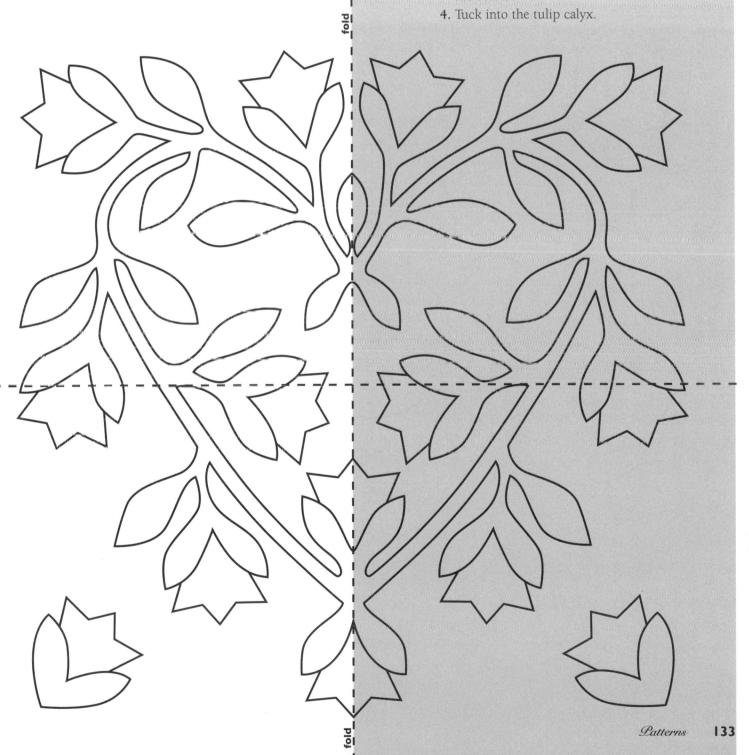

Hearts and Leaves Papercut

Symbolism

With hearts and a richness of leaves, this could be a token of affection.

Vintage Inscription

This patch—compassion—friendship and esteem,

Mingling with many as a token,

That Friendship's ties are yet unbroken.

—Antique quilt block inscription

Examples

See quilts on pages 37, 38, 40, 41, and 43.

Pattern Note

This block is taught in Lesson 2 (page 56).

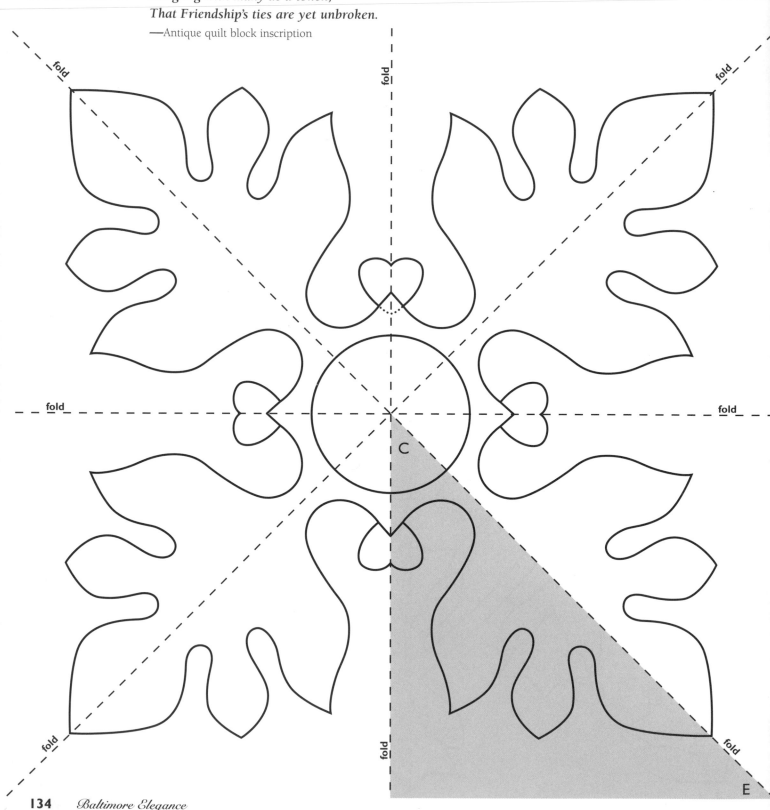

Oak Leaves and Reel Papercut *(Plain or Fancy)*

Symbolism

Acorns—Longevity; Oak tree—Strength against adversity; Reel—Venerable pattern motif (The reel was a common household object in the olden days—a device for winding, and thus thriftily saving, wool, rags, string, and so on.)

Examples

See quilts on pages 36, 37, 40, and 43.

Pattern Note

This pattern is taught in Lesson 1 (page 47).

Vintage Inscription

While I my needle ply with skill
With mimic flowers my canvas fill
O may I often raise
My thoughts to Him who made the flowers
And gave us all that we call ours
And render youthful praise.

—1803 needlework inscription

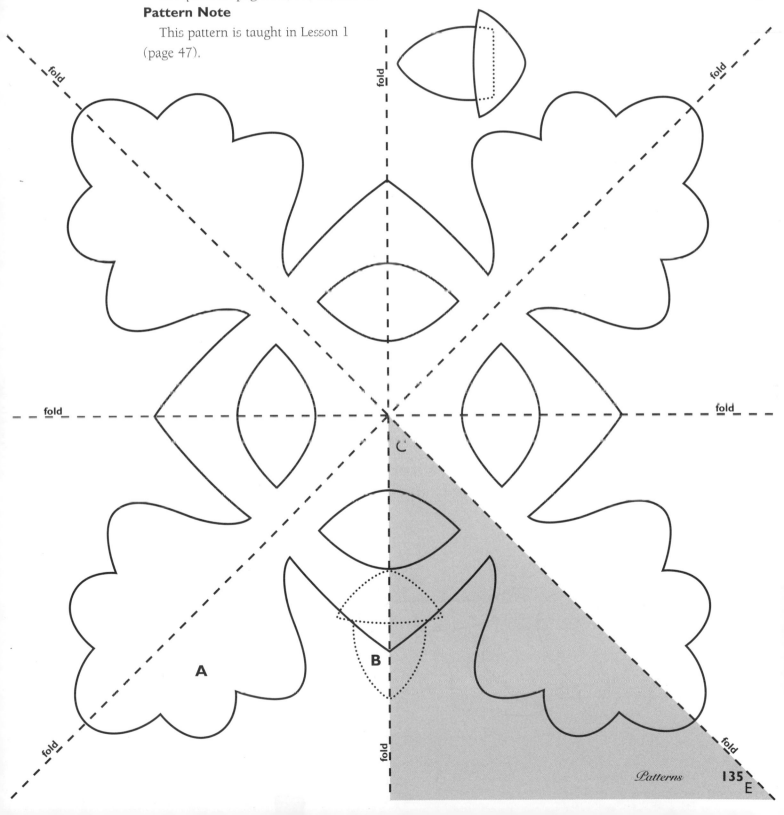

Wife, Mother, Sister, Daughter, Aunt

Symbolism

Apple—Perpetual concord; Tulip—Renown, fame; Cherry twins—Love's charms, good luck symbol

Vintage Inscription

Above my head,
Where no one can see,
My Guardian Angel,
Watches over me.

Examples

See quilts on pages 35, 36, 39, 42, and 44.

Pattern Notes

Beverly Gamble used Ultrasuede (page 60) for the head (penning in the details with a Pigma pen) and calyxes; she fused (page 33) and blanket-stitched the fruit and flowers; and she used oil pastel to shade (page 72) the apple. Simple techniques that are wondrously effective!

Husband, Father, Brother, Son, Uncle

Symbolism

We'll take the meaning from a Sweet William—Gallantry, finesse, flawlessness

Vintage Inscription

Praising what is lost makes the remembrance dear.

—William Shakespeare

Examples

See quilts on pages 35, 36, 39, 42, and 44.

Pattern Notes

Beverly Gamble cut the face, hair, and neck as one piece of Ultrasuede and used colored Pigma .01 pens to ink in the details. She cut the hands, feet, and calyxes from Ultrasuede (page 60), fused the leaves (page 33), and made up charming Pleated Flowers.

See page 147 for instructions on making the Pleated Flowers.

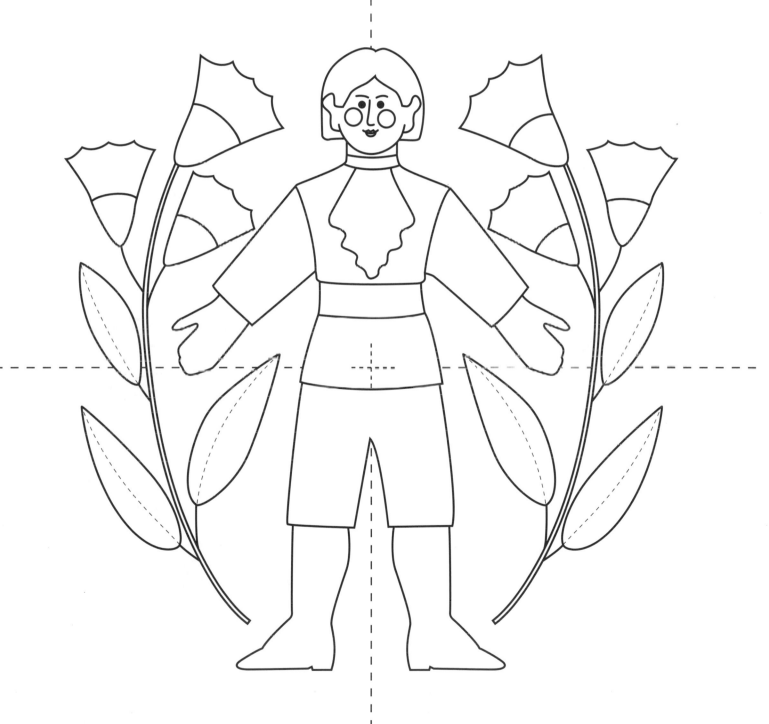

Starburst

Symbolism

Star—Divine guidance

Vintage Inscription

Of female arts in usefulness
The needle far exceeds the rest,
In ornament there's no device
Affords adornings half so nice.

While thus we practice every art
To adorn and grace our mortal part
Let us with no less care devise
To improve the mind that never dies.

—1802 needlework inscription

Examples

See quilts on pages 38, 39, 41, 43, and 44.

Pattern Notes

Trace the foliage clockwise, quadrant by quadrant, onto an 8″ × 8″ freezer-paper square folded into quadrants. Transfer the foliage first, by Freezer Paper on Top, using pattern bridges.

Trace the star onto the top fold of a 5″ × 5″ freezer-paper square folded into quadrants. The dotted lines at the center suggest a place to inscribe the block (pages 71–72). This could be done before the appliqué.

Kathy Gerardi added an inner circle of appliqué and a charming leafed bloom for the three-leafed cluster (see her quilt on page 43).

fold

Temporary Pattern Bridge

Temporary Pattern Bridge

fold

fold

fold

Star With Tulips

Symbolism

Stars—Divine guidance; Tulips—Renown, fame

Vintage Inscription

Silently, one by one,
In the infinite meadows of heaven
Blossomed the lovely stars,
The forget-me-nots of angels.

Examples

See quilts on pages 37, 40, 43, and 44.

Pattern Notes

Trace the foliage A with pattern bridges onto an 8″ × 8″ freezer-paper square folded into quadrants.

Trace the star B onto the top fold of a 5″ × 5″ freezer-paper square folded into quadrants.

Suggested approach: Do foliage A by pattern-bridged Cutaway Appliqué; use Freezer Paper on Top for star B (leave D open to the background or back with another color); do C as Separate Unit Appliqués With Freezer Paper Inside.

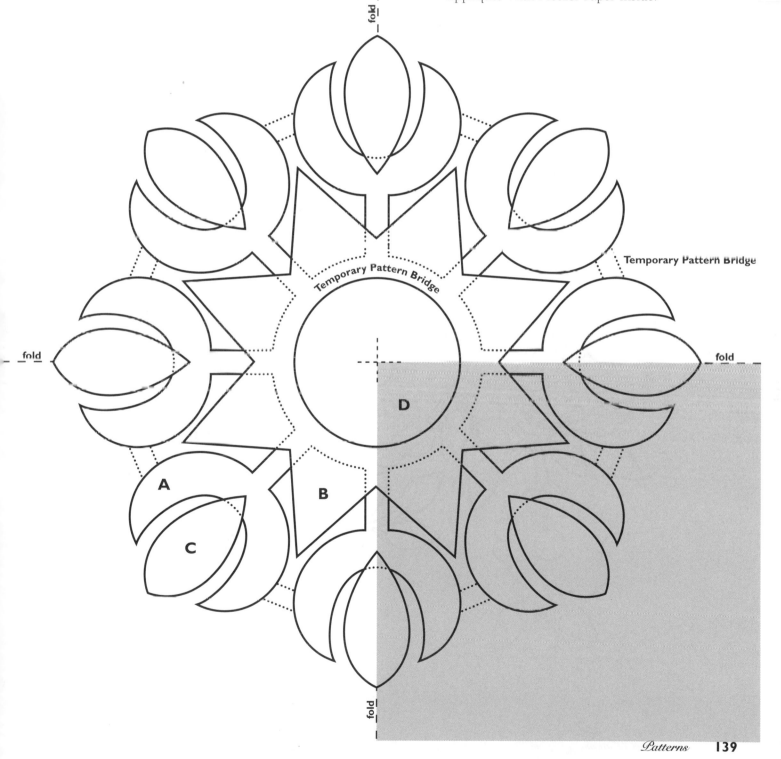

Star Rose

Symbolism

Star—Divine guidance; Rose—Love

Vintage Inscription

When with the needle I'm employed
Or whatsoever I pursue
Teach me O Thou Almighty Lord
To keep my final end in view.

—1809 needlework inscription

Examples

See quilts on pages 36, 41, 42, and 44.

Pattern Notes

The appliquéd large and medium stems can be pattern bridged in the manner of Lesson 5.

The smallest stems are embroidered (draw their placement with single lines); the leaves can be done with Freezer Paper on Top or Inside over a minimally marked background (pages 117–118).

The needleartists have done the flowers by two-layer appliqué, shell ruching, and star ruching. For ruching, mark only the rose center on the background.

See page 147 for instructions on Star Ruching.

Flower B

Flower A

PATTERN
21

Squirrel's Berry Breakfast

Symbolism

Squirrel—Thriftiness

Vintage Inscription

Please to survey this with a tender eye
Put on good nature and lay judgment by.

—1815 needlework inscription

Examples

Beverly Gamble (page 42) filled the circles—raspberry-like—with French knots! Bette Augustine created her quilt's center medallion (page 41) by repeating this block four times around the star from Pattern 19: Star With Tulips. She added small stars (Template A—see page 146)) on the lowest branch, left and right, and fringed roses on the remaining six branches.

Pattern Notes

Use pattern-bridged Cutaway Appliqué, as in Lesson 5, and do the circles as in Lesson 6.

Do the squirrel as Separate Unit Appliqué.

See page 148 for instructions on making the Fringed Roses

Family Tree House

Symbolism

Birds—Life of the soul

Bird nest, eggs—New birth, children

Inscription

Donna Bailey (page 35) inscribed this block "Samantha Hope Bailey—born February 11, 2002" and pictured Father above and Mother below.

Examples

See quilts on pages 35, 36, 41, 42, and 44.

Pattern Notes

Trace the tree onto an 8″ × 8″ freezer-paper square folded into quadrants.

Do the birds and nest as Separate Unit Appliqué. Consider using a photocopied transparency overlay for pattern placement.

Bette Augustine chain-stitched the small branches and made this tree's blossoms with what we'll call Bette's Most Amazing Fringed Flowers.

See page 149 for instructions on Bette's Fringed Flowers.

Katya Sienkiewicz   Born September 17, 1977!

Tree of Life

Symbolism

Genesis 2:9: And out of the ground made the Lord God to grow every tree that is pleasant to the sight, and good for food; the tree of life also in the midst of the garden, and the tree of knowledge of good and evil.

Revelation 14: Blessed are they that do His commandments, that they may have right to the tree of life, and may enter in through the gates into the city.

Inscription

May you grow old sharing the same pillow.
May the joys of today be the joys of tomorrow.
And may your joys well outweigh your sorrows.
—Wedding blessing

Examples

See quilts on pages 38, 39, 42, 43, and 44.

Pattern Notes

Trace pattern onto an 8″ × 8″ freezer-paper square folded into quadrants.

Family History Block

So called because it is an open invitation to record some precious information about your family's story.

Symbolism

The antique original had palmettos in the large triangles, symbols of creative power and peace.

Vintage Inscription

Count the day lost
Whose low descending sun
Views from thy hand
No worthy action done.

Examples

See quilts on pages 37, 40, and 44.

Pattern Note

This block is taught in Lesson 4 (page 68).

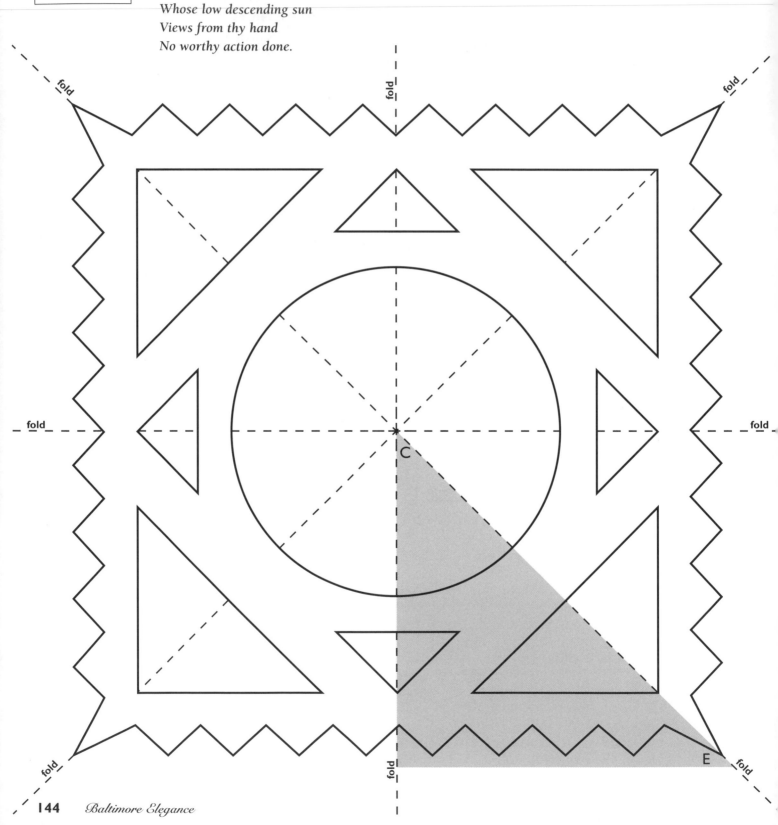

Heart and Hand Announcement ❄ ♥

Symbolism

Heart and hand—Whatsoever the hand shall do, the heart shall follow; Service and the spirit in which it is given (Oddfellows); Hands to work, and hearts to God (Shaker motto)

Vintage Inscription

Rejoice! Followed by the announcement (birth, marriage, graduation)

Examples

See quilt on page 44.

Pattern Notes

Suggested approach:

1. Inscribe the announcements (pages 71–72).
2. Appliqué the heart and the hand.
3. Make a freezer-paper Cutaway Appliqué pattern for the frame.
4. Iron the frame centered on a 9″ × 9″ square of appliqué fabric.
5. Center, pin, baste, and then appliqué the frame over the background.

fold

fold

fold

fold

fold

fold

REJOICE!

JANA & COLTER
SIENKIEWICZ

BORN MARCH 20+
MAY 23, 2005

C

Additional Pattern Pieces

Template Pattern A: Star Flower

Pattern 21: Squirrel's Berry Breakfast (page 141)

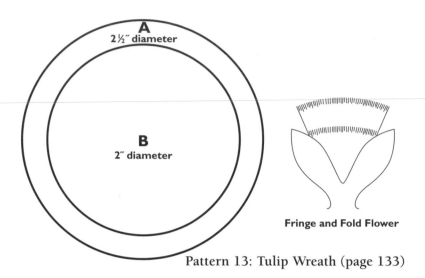

A
2½″ diameter

B
2″ diameter

Fringe and Fold Flower

Pattern 13: Tulip Wreath (page 133)

Make a Yo-Yo Rose

See Pattern 10 on page 130.

1. Cut a circle using Template A (2″ diameter circle) for a ¾″ diameter yo-yo.

2. Turn a ¼″ hem to the wrong side. With a running stitch midway between the fold and the raw edge, make ¼″ pleats (2–3 at a time). Pull to gather them until you come full circle. Continue to stitch back through the first 3 pleats, then secure the thread.

3. To fringe the center, cut a circle with Template B. Fringe the circle by pulling threads out of the edge with a needle and tweezers. Fold the circle into eighths. Use embroidery scissors to tuck the circle down into the yo-yo.

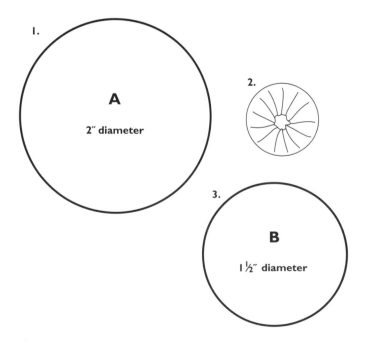

I.

A
2″ diameter

2.

3.

B
1½″ diameter

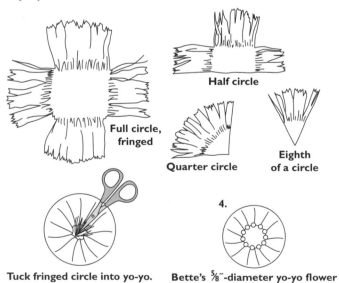

Half circle

Full circle,
fringed

Quarter circle

Eighth
of a circle

Tuck fringed circle into yo-yo.

Bette's ⅝″-diameter yo-yo flower

4. The 1½″ circle Template B also makes ⅝″-diameter yo-yos. These center the ruched roses on Beverly Gamble's Star Rose block. Bette Augustine covered her Template B unhemmed yo-yo with a ¼″ circle (gathered over hole-punched label paper, which was left in after appliqué, and wreathed it with gold French knots).

Pleated Flowers

See Pattern 17 on page 137.

1. Cut a 1″ × 2½″ rectangle.
2. Iron under a ⅛″ seam allowance at the top and on the left and right sides.
3. Mark dots for the solid lines (mountain folds) and dotted lines (valley folds) across the top. Do the same across the bottom. Iron 5 pleats from the top hemmed edge to the bottom raw edge. (It may help to fold this in graph paper first.)
4. Make a fan, tucking the raw edge under the tulip calyx. Pin, baste, and appliqué in place beneath the tulip calyx.

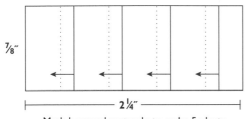

⅞″

2¼″

Mark hemmed rectangle to make 5 pleats.
Press folds to the left.

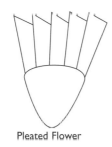

Pleated Flower

Star Ruching

See Pattern 20 on page 140.

A quilter graciously sent me a template shape for ruching done in the shape of a star. But she did not include her name. The star shape ruches magically, and I see Pattern 20 as its perfect place to bloom.

1. Trace star Templates A and B onto fabric. Cut them out on the drawn lines.
2. Start with a knot and sew a running stitch [c] and [b], but leave long threads for gathering.
3. Sew a running stitch [a] and pull to gather until 6 even petals are formed. The circle edge will have turned under to form a roughly ⅛″ seam allowance. Secure and then cut the thread.

4. Gather circle [b], then [c]. When the center flattens, secure and then cut the threads.
5. Arrange the petals, pin, baste, and then appliqué the star rose to the background. Optionally, you could embroider French knots in its center.

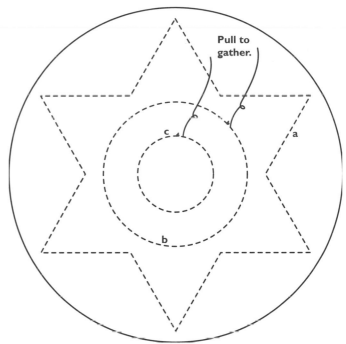

Pull to gather.

Large Star Rose Ruching Template A

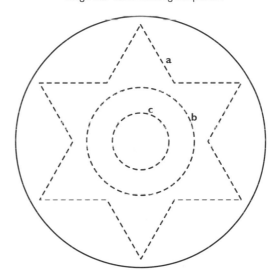

Small Star Rose Ruching Template B

Gathered star rose appliquéd to background

Fringed Roses

See Pattern 21 on page 14.

Here, Bette Augustine shares how to make her Fringed Roses.

THE FRINGED CIRCLE

1. Cut a 1″ × 5″ strip on the grain. Fold it in half lengthwise, right sides together.
2. Running stitch the fold close to the edge between [a] and [b]. Pull to gather. Stitch [a] to [b]. Secure the stitches.

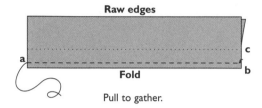

Pull to gather.

3. Use tweezers to pull the threads to fringe between the raw edge and a line [c] ⅛″ above the gathering line.

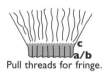

Pull threads for fringe.

4. Flatten the gathered circle and tack stitch the intact fabric ring [d] to the background where you want to place the fringed rose.

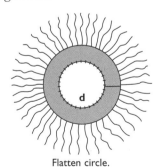

Flatten circle.

THE ROSE-LIKE CENTER

1. Cut a bias strip 1″ × 4″. Fold it in half lengthwise. Sew a running stitch as close to the raw edges as you can, catching the right corner in the gather line (this will become the rose center [a]).

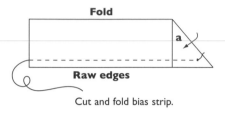

Cut and fold bias strip.

2. Pull to gather the strip.

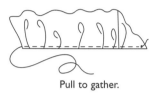

Pull to gather.

3. Roll the raw edge into a flower shape fitted to the center of your fringed circle. Hide the end underneath and tack it on the underside to hold its shape.

Roll.

4. Stitch the rolled rose shape into the center of the circle. Bette notes that it should be loose (not gathered so tightly as to stand up stiffly) along its outside edge to create a flower center.

Fringed Rose

Bette's Most Amazing Fringed Flowers

See Pattern 22 on page 142.

1. Cut a 1″-diameter circle from your flower fabric [a].
2. From self-stick label paper, cut (or hole punch) a ⅜″ circle [b]. Stick it centered over the wrong side of the flower fabric.
3. Sew a running stitch in a circle ⅛″ outside and parallel to the paper center [c]. Pull the gathers tightly. Secure the thread and cut.

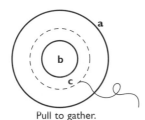

Pull to gather.

4. You've made a pouch [d]. The paper is inside and stays there forever (quoth Bette).

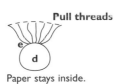

Paper stays inside.

5. Pull out the threads down to the gather line [e] to make the fringe.
6. Push down to open the center. Stitch a colonial knot in the center (3 strands, 3 wraps; see page 32). Appliqué the base to the background. Bette suggests taking a little white glue on your fingertip and dabbing it under the fringe to stiffen it to stand up from the background in a halo-like fringe.

Finished blossom with colonial knot center

Wreath of Holly

Made by Mary K. Tozer (see page 45)

Symbolism

Wreath of holly—Foresight and defense, Christ's crown of thorns, the Passion, Christmas (Christian)

Vintage Inscription

Make it your ambition to lead a peaceful and quiet life and to work with your hands.

—I Thessalonians 4:11

Pattern Notes

See page 115 for enlargement percentages. Mary needleturned this plethora of berries with grace and patience!

fold

fold

fold

fold

The Bricklayer's House

Made by Mercy Arrastia (see page 45)

Symbolism

Crown of roses—Superior merit

An open wreath is called a crown, as in an Olympian's crown of laurel.

Vintage Inscription

My Love for thee, like roses,
Blooms within my heart
And like their lovely fragrance
Never will depart.

Pattern Notes

See page 115 for enlargement percentages.

Though now discredited, many such fancy blocks were at one time attributed to Mary Evans (a name connected tangentially in the *William Rush Dunton Notebooks*), and then to Mary Simon (because of a contemporary diarist's partial sentence reference possibly to such blocks), though this attribution is now also contested. Of interest, though, is that the original of this block is signed Mary E. Gray—one wonders if this was an early marriage for Mary Evans (later, Ford), whose father was a bricklayer. The quilt (promised gift to the Museum of Fine Arts, Houston) was made for Ebenezer Stewart, Album-era owner of Baltimore's brickyard.

A Hero's Crown (Dove and Anchor)

Made by Bette F. Augustine (see page 4) and Darla Jo Hanks (see page 46)

Symbolism

Dove—Innocence, purity, Holy Spirit, peace (Christian); Chains—The Passion, salvation (Christian); Anchor—Steadfastness, safety, protection, salvation, hope, the soul (Christian)

Vintage Inscription

Beauty and pride we often find
Betray the weakness of the mind;
He handsome is and merits praise
That handsome does, the Proverb says.

—1766 needlework inscription

Pattern Notes

See page 115 for enlargement percentages.

Darla Jo Hanks made hers a splendid 22″ medallion quilt center, beginning a quilt that will honor her son, who serves his fellow countrymen as a marine, now in Iraq. She calls her block *Truth, Honor & Commitment.*

Bette Augustine's is an exquisite 8″ miniature. The Colonial knots are stitched with 50-weight DMC machine embroidery cotton.

Lovebirds in Wreath

Made by Mercy Arrastia (see page 45)

Symbolism

Lovebirds and parakeets—Romantic love

Vintage Inscription

*The time of the singing of birds is come,
and the voice of the turtle is heard in our land.*

—The Song of Solomon

Pattern Notes

See page 115 for enlargement percentages.

The original block contained more red and yellow, which have since become mellowed by time. Mercy has reproduced the block beautifully but in the sunnier colors of Florida, where she began its stitching.

Celebrating Baltimore's Iron Horse

Made by Donna Hall Bailey (see page 46)

Symbolism

Iron Horse—Baltimore's civic pride and the Industrial Revolution

Vintage Inscription

The daily labors of the bee
Awake my soul to Industry
And from the most minute and mean
A virtuous mind can morals glean.

—1796 sampler inscription

Pattern Notes

See page 115 for enlargement percentages.

Album-makers would have remembered the famous race between Baltimore's first train, the Tom Thumb, and a horse—which won.

Baltimore Clipper Ship

Made by Mary K. Tozer (see page 46)

Symbolism

Clipper ship—Christianity, the Church, salvation (Christian)

Vintage Inscription

Teach me to feel another's woe,
To hide the fault I see;
That mercy I to others show
That mercy show to me.

—1787 sampler inscription

Pattern Notes

See page 115 for enlargement percentages.

For a while, Baltimore clipper ships were the fastest ships on the seas. The good ship *Hope* plied the waters between Baltimore and Bremen, taking over cotton and tobacco and bringing back German immigrants. Their needlework influence shows beautifully in Baltimore's Albums. Mary's background fabric ingeniously echoes billowing clouds.

Wreath of Currant Buds and Blooms

Made by Yvonne Suutari (see page 45)

Symbolism

Currants—I am worthy of you!

Vintage Inscription

Be you to others kind and true
As you would have others be to you
Nor neither do nor say to men
What you are unwilling to take again.

—1796 needlework inscription

Pattern Notes

See page 115 for enlargement percentages.

Yvonne made the tiny blossoms with fusible-backed fabric (page 33), embroidering the edge. This block, like Mary K. Tozer's (pages 45 and 150), seems to occur only once in antique Baltimore Albums, perhaps because their unique style entails such labor-intensive fine needlework!

Urn of Flowers

Made by Nadine E. Thompson (see page 46)

Symbolism

Urns—Symbol of life (and death); Urn of flowers—The sweet soul ascending to heaven

Vintage Inscription

By virtue ripened from the bud
The flowers angelic odors breathe,
The fragrant charm of being good
Makes gaudy vice to smell like weeds.

—Ethel Stanton Bolton

A life beyond the veil of heaven.

—as seen in draped urns in Victorian graveyards

Pattern Notes

See page 115 for enlargement percentages

As I drafted this interpreted block from the Baltimore Museum of Art's Samuel Williams Quilt, the original design seemed mysteriously antiquarian. Why the six-pointed star flower and the nonbotanical bloom beneath it? Why the spiky rigid stems so carefully crossing above the Greek-style drinking-cup vase? Mystery, though, is part of Baltimore's intrigue. Nadine—like a fine painter—has caught the original's evocative beauty, mystery and all!

BORDER PATTERNS

These border pattern motifs are all scaled to fit the smaller Baltimore Album blocks in this book.

Karen Evans's Center-Running Borders

See *Basic Baltimore: Angel to Come* page 40.

Karen's exquisite quilt could be considered in the tradition of strippy quilts—quilt motifs set in vertical rows separated by sashings, rather than set in grids. Her quilt's title, *Basic Baltimore: Angel to Come*, bespeaks great expectations!

Janet Costello's Hearts and Roses Border

See *Family* on page 36.

The Trifold Stem method (page 90) would be excellent for this stem. Note that Janet made the rosebud stems from six strands of floss, using the stem stitch.

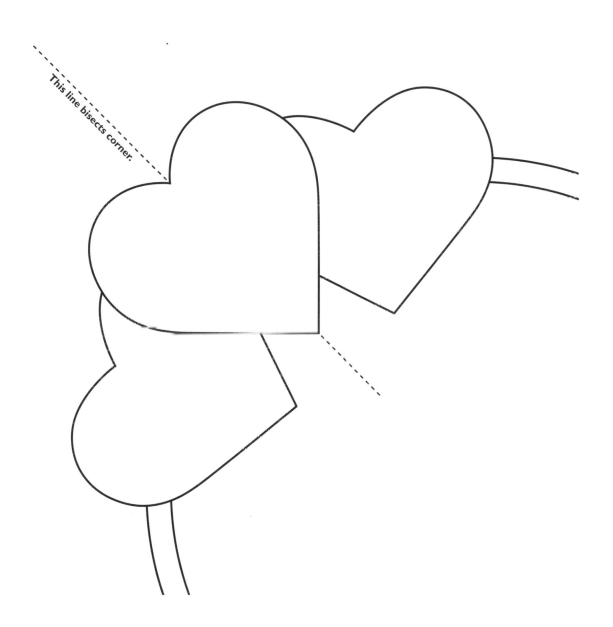

This line bisects corner.

Border center

Bette F. Augustine's Stars and Flowers Border

See *Quiet Moments* on page 41.

Bette adapted Block Pattern 21: Squirrel's Berry Breakfast to make the center medallion and this border. She enlarged the center star from Pattern 18:

Starburst for the center medallion, and she used the Pattern 21 foliage for both the medallion and the border.

Center line

Join along this line to complete border section.

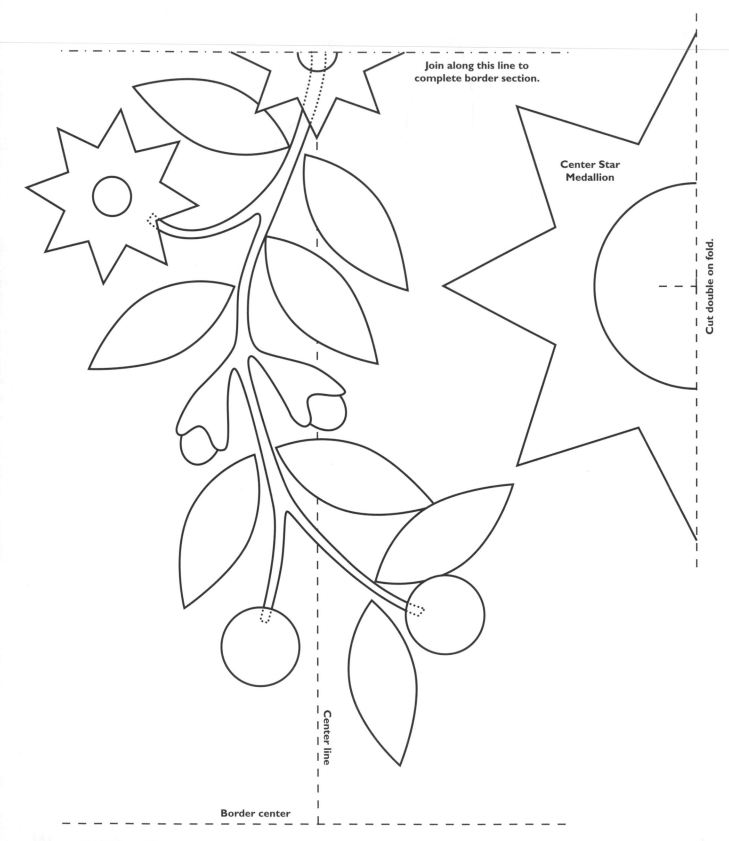

BORDER PATTERN *3*

Join along this line to complete border section.

Center Star Medallion

Cut double on fold.

Center line

Border center

Kathy Rankin's Swag Border

See *Baby Baltimore* on page 38.

This border is adapted from my *Appliqué 12 Borders and Medallions*. Kathy reduced the swag 50% to fit her smaller-size quilt. Then she used flowers from Block Pattern 2: Crossed Flowers (page 122) to join the swag pieces and for the corner border flowers.

Cut double on fold for swag.

Corner flower

Michele Silberhorn's Rose-Held Swag Border

See *Baby, Oh Baby, Baby Baltimore* on page 44.

Michele adapted this border from my *Appliqué 12 Borders and Medallions*. She created a small flower to fit over the swags.

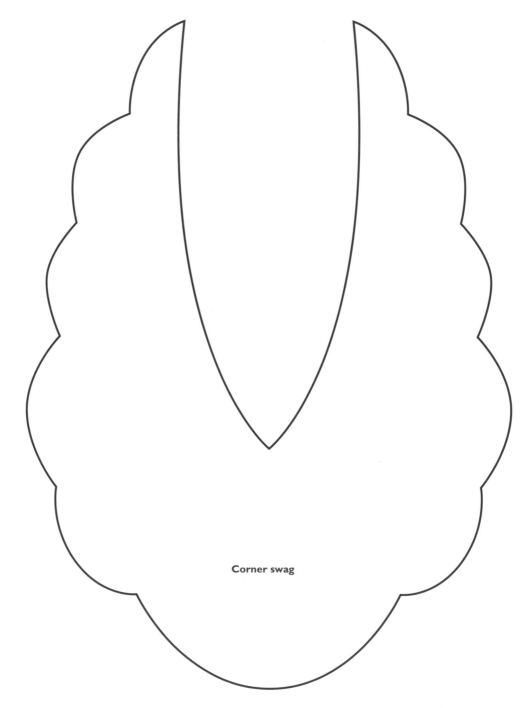

Corner swag

Cut double on fold for swag.

Kathy Gerardi's Star Rose Border

See *For Edna and Kathryn* on page 43.

This elegant diva shines forth not only as a block but also as a border in Kathy Gerardi's quilt. Repeated four times, the Star Rose makes a dramatic center medallion in Janet Costello's quilt (page 36). Stars have captured the imaginations of many artists, whether quiltmakers or bards:

"There was a star danced, and under that was I born." —*King Henry V*, Shakespeare.

Even constructing the Star Rose evokes creativity. I interpreted the rose with Star Ruching (page 147), while several needleartists used Shell Ruching (page 80).

Corner

Angie Witting's Dancing Grapevine Border With Half-Triangle Sashing

See To Chris With Love on page 44.

Angie chose an elegant border to complete her lovely quilt. Use the Trifold Stem method (page 90) to make its meandering vine; embroider the grape stems and tendrils.

The Dancing Grapevine is an original pattern I designed for *Appliqué 12 Borders and Medallions*. Here is the pattern for Angie's miniaturized adaptation.

Border center

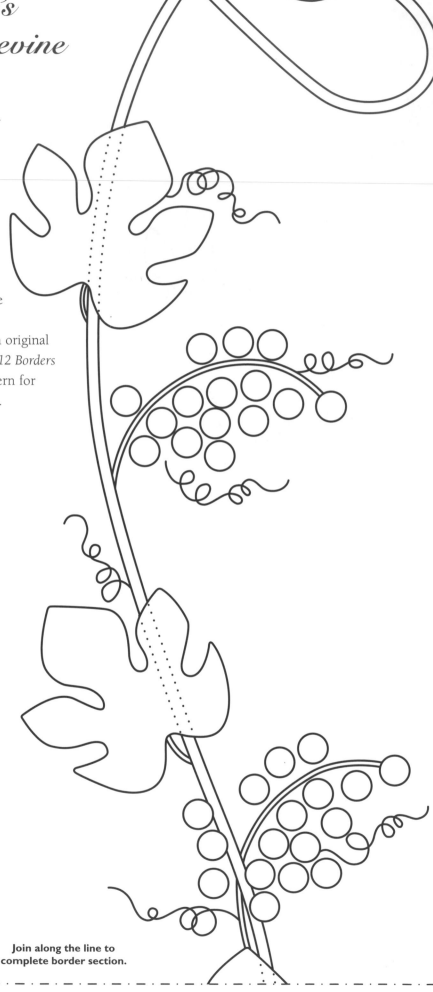

Join along the line to complete border section.

Join along the line to complete border section.

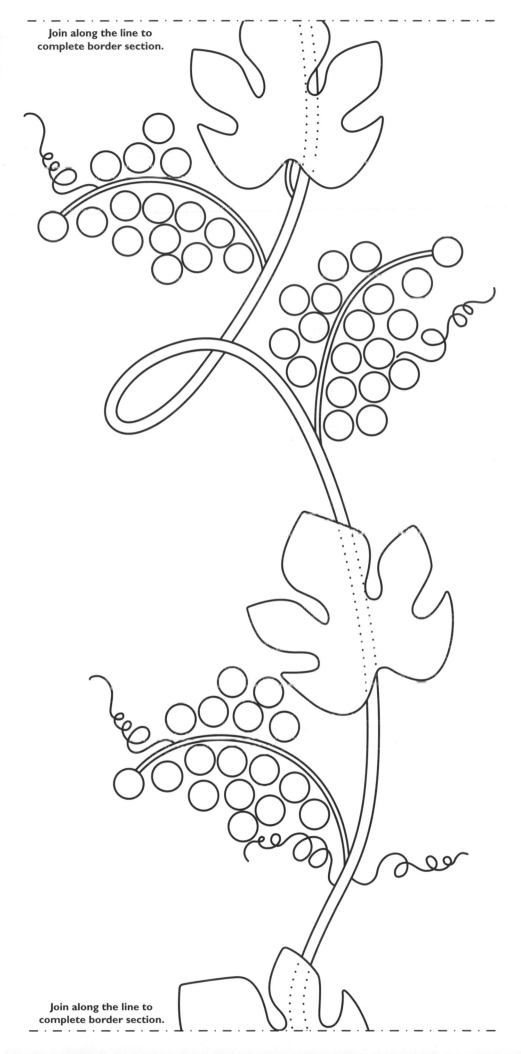

Join along the line to complete border section.

Join along the line to complete border section.

$1\frac{7}{8}''$ $\frac{1}{4}''$

Make 99 copies of the pattern for the half-square triangle sashing.

Lynda Carswell's Sashing and Setting Star

See *Suite Baby Baltimore* on page 37.

These instructions are for a nine-block quilt (3 × 3) using the smaller (8″ finished) Baltimore Album blocks in this book.

Cutting

From the sashing fabric:
Cut 18 strips 1″ × 8½″.
Cut 18 strips 1″ × 9½″.
Cut 96 squares 1¼″ × 1¼″.
Cut 4 strips 2″ × the width of the fabric for the outside border.

From the background fabric:
Cut 24 rectangles 2″ × 9½″.
Cut 16 squares 2″ × 2″.

Making the Border

1. Sew a 1″ × 8½″ sashing strip to opposite sides of each appliqué block. Press.
2. Sew a 1″ × 9½″ sashing strip to the remaining sides of the blocks. Press.
3. Draw a diagonal line on each square from corner to corner. Sew the squares on the drawn line to the ends of the 2″ × 9½″ rectangles. Trim the seam allowances. Press.
4. Sew 4 sashing rectangles to 3 blocks to make 3 rows of blocks. Press toward the blocks.
5. Sew 4 background squares to 3 sashing rectangles to make 4 rows of sashing. Press toward the squares.
6. Sew alternate rows of sashing and blocks together. Press.
7. Add the outside borders. Press toward the border.

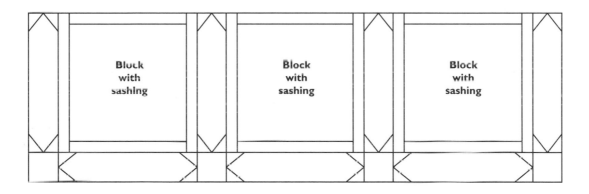

Dogtooth and Star Border

See *Marlena* on page 39 and *Baby Blue—Baby Baltimore* on page 42.

The fabric for Lee Snow and Marjorie Lydecker's *Marlena* border (from my *Baltimore Beauties III* fabric collection) was designed to coordinate and is skillfully used. Noteworthy is the eye-catching pattern created by using two different background fabrics. The outer border is created using the Dogtooth Border method (see Lesson 4, pages 69–70).

Beverly Gamble's border in *Baby Blue–Baby Baltimore* is another example of the Dogtooth Border method.

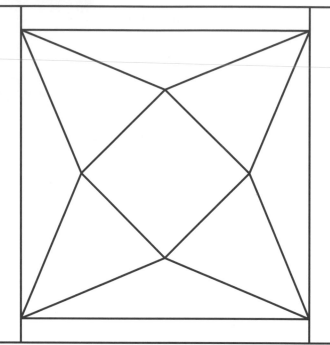

Corner Star Block

Nancy Wakefield's Star Block Pattern

See *United We Stand* on page 43.

The dramatic 3″ finished sashing on the quilt is made of three strips cut 1½″ wide × the width of the fabric.

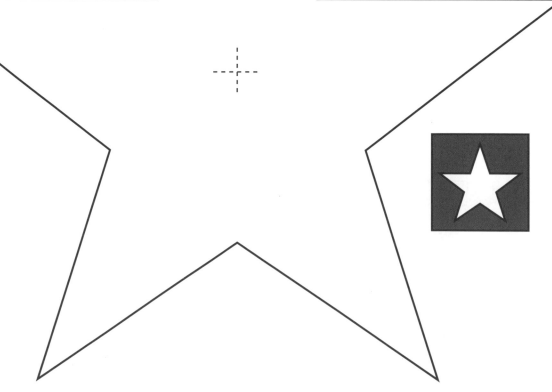

Courses and Sources

Courses

The C&T Publishing website provides lesson plans, inviting you to teach from *Baltimore Elegance* and other C&T books. I welcome teaching from my books, and many, including this one, have been written specifically as textbooks to teach yourself or to use to teach others. *Baltimore Elegance* has six lessons—an ideal number of classes for a shop or other forum.

Each lesson teaches one complete block, then enriches that basic lesson with additional patterns for more practice. This is a good beginner's course, but intermediate and advanced appliquérs also love working with these patterns. The C&T website course description details two 3-hour introductory sessions (by hand or machine) and a 1 day advanced class. As required by the copyright, students make their own patterns from the book and bring it to class.

Sources

The Elly Sienkiewicz Appliqué Academy
www.EllySienkiewicz.com
Send $2.00 for current event brochure (mails late July). The annual academy, held the third week in February in Colonial Williamsburg, Virginia, is for all appliquérs, from beginners to advanced. It features ten excellent national teachers, fun, and fellowship!
Send your requests to
Bette Augustine, Administrator
41195 Toledo Drive
Hemet, CA 93544
951-658-4260
email: bette@ellysienkiewicz.com
Elly would love to come teach at your guild or conference. Her teaching schedule is posted on her website. Bette will forward your emailed teaching inquiry to Elly.

Robert Kaufman Fabrics
www.robertkaufman.com
For Elly Sienkiewicz's *Beyond Baltimore* and *Spoken Without a Word* designer fabric lines from Robert Kaufman Fabrics, visit your local quilt shop, or check the Robert Kaufman website to see both of Elly's lines (under Quilts) and to find retail outlets.

Mare's Bears Quilt Shop
www.maresbearsquiltshop.com
An ocean resort destination. For Elly's designer fabrics (from Robert Kaufman), books, and information about Appliqué by the Bay, where Elly teaches annually the first week of December, and for Printed Treasures Printer Fabric Sheets.
Maryann McFee
528 Savannah Road
Lewes, DE 19958
302-644-0556
email: maresbears@ce.net

Nutmeg Lodge Shop
www.nutmeglodge.com
For Elly's books and fabric
Barbara Lee Bradley 304-262-6633

Quilt Adventures
www.quiltadventures.com
For Elly's designer fabrics and books, Ultrasuede, kitted blocks, Baltimore Reproduction Challenge blocks, Thread Gatherer hand-dyed silk ribbons and flosses, and the latest in quilt supplies.
Cynthia Williford
596 E. Danskin Drive
Boise, ID 83716
877-360-6300 (toll free) or 208-433-8587
email: cynthia@quiltadventures.com

The Graham Cracker Collection, Inc.
www.grahamcrackercollection.com
For additional delightful projects and patterns by Janice Vaine, the guest artist project designer for *Baltimore Elegance*.
Janice Vaine
1730 Shadowood Lane, Suite 320
Jacksonville, FL 32207
904-725-7499
email:grahamcrackercollection@comcast.net

Heartbeat Quilts
A Cape Cod resort destination where Elly teaches annually. A mega-quiltshop (include it in your shopping for Elly's fabrics) with a must-read newsletter.

Helen Weinman
765 Main Street
Hyannis, MA 02601
508-771-0011 or 800-393-8050
Fax: 508-790-2711
email: QuiltHelen@aol.com

The Twining Thread
www.twiningthread.com
Shop this website for a plethora of wired and velvet ribbon, fancy flosses, wool felt, and embroidery books.
The Twining Thread
P.O. Box 485
Newport OR 97365-0033
541-265-2166

Leo9 Textiles
For 8½˝ square rulers to trim finished blocks
email: leo9@smithsys.net

Basic Quilting Books

All About Quilting from *Quilter's Newsletter Magazine, Quiltmaker Magazine,* and C&T Publishing
Quilts, Quilts, and More Quilts by Diana McClun and Laura Nownes
Rotary Cutting With Alex Anderson by Alex Anderson
Start Quilting With Alex Anderson by Alex Anderson

For more information about these and other books ask for a free catalog:
C&T Publishing, Inc.
P.O. Box 1456
Lafayette, CA 94549
800-284-1114
email: ctinfo@ctpub.com
www.ctpub.com

Quilting Supplies

Cotton Patch Mail Order
3404 Hall Lane
Dept. CTB
Lafayette, CA 94549
800-835-4418 or 925-283-7883
email: quiltusa@yahoo.com
www.quiltusa.com

Note: Fabrics used in the quilts shown may not be currently available because fabric manufacturers keep most fabrics in print for only a short time.

About the Author

Elly Sienkiewicz lives in Washington, D.C., with her husband. Their three children, so young when she started quiltmaking and writing books, are now grown and have children of their own.

Elly has written nineteen books, all of which have been connected to teaching and to appliqué. Her impact on the Baltimore Album revival is undeniable. She has been sharing her knowledge and enthusiasm for these quilts for more than twenty years, and she hopes appliqué and needlework bring you the peace and pleasure they have brought her.

Other Books by Elly Sienkiewicz

Currently available

Baltimore Beauties and Beyond, Volume One

Appliqué 12 Easy Ways

Sweet Dreams, Moon Baby

The Best of Baltimore Beauties

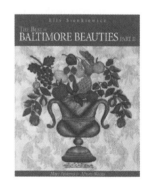

The Best of Baltimore Beauties, Part II

Also by Elly Sienkiewicz

Appliqué 12 Borders and Medallions
Appliqué a Paper Greeting
Appliqué a Paper Greeting and Scrapbooking
Baltimore Album Legacy
Baltimore Album Quilts
Baltimore Album Revival
Baltimore Beauties and Beyond, Volume Two

Baltimore Beauties and Beyond, Volume Three
Design a Baltimore Album Quilt
Dimensional Appliqué
Papercuts and Plenty
Romancing Ribbons Into Flowers
Spoken Without a Word

Index

Baltimore Elegance Blocks

Reproduction Blocks

Pattern Transfer Methods

Quilts

Great Titles from C&T PUBLISHING

Hand Appliqué with ALEX ANDERSON
Host of Simply Quilts as seen on HGTV

SEVEN PROJECTS FOR HAND APPLIQUÉ

CAROL ARMSTRONG
Kitty Capers
15 Quilt Projects with Purrsonality

The New Appliqué Sampler
Learn to Appliqué the Piece O' Cake Way

BECKY GOLDSMITH & LINDA JENKINS

Appliqué Delights
100 IRRESISTIBLE BLOCKS
from Piece O' Cake Designs

BECKY GOLDSMITH & LINDA JENKINS

Available at your local retailer or
www.ctpub.com or 800.284.1114